Cambridge Elements ≡

Elements in New Religious Movements
Series Editor
Rebecca Moore
San Diego State University
Founding Editor
†James R. Lewis
Wuhan University

NEW RELIGIOUS MOVEMENTS AND COMPARATIVE RELIGION

Olav Hammer
University of Southern Denmark

Karen Swartz-Hammer
Åbo Akademi University

CAMBRIDGE
UNIVERSITY PRESS

Shaftesbury Road, Cambridge CB2 8EA, United Kingdom

One Liberty Plaza, 20th Floor, New York, NY 10006, USA

477 Williamstown Road, Port Melbourne, VIC 3207, Australia

314–321, 3rd Floor, Plot 3, Splendor Forum, Jasola District Centre, New Delhi – 110025, India

103 Penang Road, #05–06/07, Visioncrest Commercial, Singapore 238467

Cambridge University Press is part of Cambridge University Press & Assessment, a department of the University of Cambridge.

We share the University's mission to contribute to society through the pursuit of education, learning and research at the highest international levels of excellence.

www.cambridge.org
Information on this title: www.cambridge.org/9781009500746

DOI: 10.1017/9781009029469

When citing this work, please include a reference to the DOI 10.1017/9781009029469

First published 2024

A catalogue record for this publication is available from the British Library.

ISBN 978-1-009-50074-6 Hardback
ISBN 978-1-009-01459-5 Paperback
ISSN 2635-232X (online)
ISSN 2635-2311 (print)

Cambridge University Press & Assessment has no responsibility for the persistence or accuracy of URLs for external or third-party internet websites referred to in this publication and does not guarantee that any content on such websites is, or will remain, accurate or appropriate.

New Religious Movements and Comparative Religion

Elements in New Religious Movements

DOI: 10.1017/9781009029469
First published online: January 2024

Olav Hammer
University of Southern Denmark

Karen Swartz-Hammer
Åbo Akademi University

Author for correspondence: Olav Hammer, ohammer@sdu.dk

Abstract: This Element provides an introduction to a number of less frequently explored approaches based upon the comparative study of religions. New religions convey origin myths, present their particular views of history, and craft Endtime scenarios. Their members carry out a vast and diverse array of ritual activities. They produce large corpuses of written texts and designate a subset of these as a sacrosanct canon. They focus their attention on material objects that can range from sacred buildings to objects from the natural world that are treated in ritualized fashion. The reason for this fundamental similarity between older and newer religions is briefly explored in terms of the cognitive processes that underlie religious concepts and practices. A final section returns to the issue of how such shared processes take specific shapes in the context of modern, Western societies.

Keywords: comparative religion, modern myths, rituals, material religion, sacred texts

ISBNs: 9781009500746 (HB), 9781009014595 (PB), 9781009029469 (OC)
ISSNs: 2635-232X (online), 2635-2311 (print)

Contents

Introduction

The study of new religious movements (NRMs) was born at a time when much of the West found itself in the grip of a rising moral panic.[1] Most of Europe and North America had majority Christian populations, but, by the 1960s, globalization and countercultural impulses had begun to alter the cultural landscape in increasingly noticeable ways, including the rise of a number of highly visible new religions, such as Scientology, the Hare Krishna movement (ISKCON), the Children of God, and the Unification Church. In a sense, this development was nothing new. Religious creativity was flourishing for generations prior to the appearance of these recent arrivals, and observers of the cultural scene could have pointed at numerous movements, like Spiritualism, Theosophy, Christian Science, and the Jehovah's Witnesses, as examples of such predecessors. Christianity itself, of course, was once a new and controversial religion during its formative years nearly two millennia ago (see, e.g., Hammer & Rothstein 2023) and has since that time spawned innumerable, and initially unfamiliar, offshoots. Religious innovation, in other words, is a perennial and ubiquitous phenomenon. Such facts, however, are often left by the perceptual wayside when potential threats are sensed, and thus the new religions of the post–Second World War era provoked various, and frequently negative, reactions among the general public. Concerned parents of young converts, Christian apologetic writers, and representatives of the media painted them up as decidedly bizarre and nefarious cults, and a common argument made by the critics of these newcomers was that they were so brazenly different from the more established religions that they must have made use of extraordinary methods for recruitment. Perhaps, according to this line of reasoning, these organizations had developed particularly effective brainwashing techniques for luring the innocent and unaware into their clutches (see, e.g., Introvigne 2022). Some critics believed that cult members had become so bereft of the ability to draw upon the powers of their own free will that being subjected to a regime of deprogramming, which might involve such elements as abduction and being held in isolation, was the only way to liberate them.

By the mid-1960s, approaches of a more academic provenance aiming to understand these movements had begun to take form, and, perhaps unsurprisingly, they tended to concentrate on coming to grips with what were then the most pressing questions provoked by these developments. The study of new religions was thus from its earliest days heavily oriented toward a particular set of sociological approaches and focused on such themes as recruitment patterns

---

[1] The indispensable monograph discussing the origins and development of the study of new religious movements is Ashcraft (2018).

and conflicts with mainstream society. That the area came to be dominated by this specific set of approaches had nothing to do with any kind of inherent logical necessity; instead, historical contingencies led to a particular mode of investigating new religions establishing itself as the self-evident choice.

At the time of this writing, more than half a century has passed since the field was established, and the markings of such a pronounced sociological emphasis on their "otherness" are still apparent. This unmistakable slant in focus is in some respects a paradox. One of the most robust findings of research carried out on NRMs is that they largely resemble religions with a longer history and a more established presence. Approaches that treat new religions just like any other religion and hence analyze them in ways that have been staples of the comparative study of religion as a historical and cultural phenomenon are, although certainly not entirely absent, less common than perspectives mentioned earlier. The aim of the present Element is to provide an entry-level introduction to NRMs as seen through the lenses of a selection of approaches that highlight the many features that they share with historically more well-established religions. In particular, we take up examples of the ways in which the leaders and members of NRMs, just as their peers do in traditional religions, craft and disseminate myths, create and perform rituals, compose, study, and comment upon canonical texts, and, not least, manifest their presence by means of producing a material culture which can include such elements as sacred buildings as well as objects stemming from the natural world which are treated in ritualized fashion. A section is devoted to each of these topics.

Why are new and older religions similar to each other in so many ways? The concluding section of this Element will, by calling upon the cognitive science of religion (CSR) for help, offer a few possible answers to this question. Underlying this last part is the argument that the human brain is the result of a long process of evolution. According to this perspective, conceptualizations of deities are products of the human mind and hence are similar in various religions, as are the rules these suprahuman beings wish us to abide by. The comparative study of religions should, however, not just highlight their commonalities but also contribute to a greater understanding of their differences. Since religions are part and parcel of the culture of a given society, it stands to reason that they mirror particular social and historical contexts, a theme that will be briefly explored in these final pages.

In order to illustrate various points we wish to make along the way, we will make use of a mix of examples which to some extent represents our own areas of interest and expertise. The cases we present largely come from the religious landscapes of Europe and the United States. Some concern movements already studied by the first generation of NRM scholars (such as Scientology and ISKCON).

Others have to do with new religions with a historical background in late-nineteenth-century occultism (like Theosophy and Anthroposophy). Yet other cases discussed here are not, strictly speaking, part of organized new religions but instead of what sociologist Colin Campbell (1972) called the cultic milieu: ephemeral movements, unaffiliated individuals, and loosely knit networks of people whose practices and beliefs are considered heterodox by mainstream society (e.g., Flat Earth theories and Reiki healing).

Two final questions remain to be dealt with before we close this introductory section. First, how recently produced does a religion need to be in order for us to consider it as being new, and, second, which kinds of phenomena do we count as religions? The former admittedly invites a certain degree of arbitrariness. One could argue that the term "new religions" is merely another way of saying "religion in its formative stage" and then study, say, emergent Christianity in the first decades of the Common Era as an NRM. Much scholarship has, however, tended to confine the term to signifying religions of the modern age, with the Second World War often serving as a rough starting point, but this can be seen as a matter of convention rather than as a solidly argued and theoretically grounded delimitation. No essential difference, we argue, would seem to demarcate a movement that was founded a century or more ago from more recent arrivals on the scene, and our examples therefore are taken from a span of time that begins with the birth of Mormonism around 1830, and which continues to the present day.

The second question, what counts as a religion, also requires a somewhat arbitrary answer. As a very basic way of addressing it, we take religions to be socially shared practices and concepts which ultimately refer to a culturally defined suprahuman dimension. The qualification "socially shared" means that we exclude idiosyncratic ideas and behaviors belonging to the private domain of a single individual and that we consider to be religions not only structured movements one can formally join as a member, but also social formations organized in less overt ways. From this perspective, it follows that people who have read and found plausible a book about reincarnation or who have taken a course on a spiritual topic or who have participated in a Facebook group devoted to such topics or who have consulted a practitioner of a form of healing or divination, and who have done any or all of these things with no further degree of commitment, have all been at least minimally engaged with a religious practice. This broad understanding of the term "religion" also leads us to use as examples phenomena that insiders would not necessarily recognize as religion or as religious (as is the case with many of the loosely organized New Age practices) or whose spokespersons would vehemently deny are religions (as is the case with Anthroposophy). Toward the end of the last section, we will briefly return to the question of why insiders and researchers can have diametrically opposed answers to whether any given phenomenon in contemporary culture can fruitfully be understood as religion.

1 Myths

New religious movements, like their more traditional counterparts, provide narratives that elaborate upon the creation of the cosmos, the emergence over time of various cultural advances, the course of history, and the end of time. Some NRMs take as their point of departure the stories found in existing religious traditions, others draw selectively upon science and popular culture, whereas yet others promote remarkably innovative accounts. Narratives of this kind are typically labelled myths when encountered in more well-established religions, and it seems natural to use the same label to categorize structurally similar stories in NRMs. The term "myth," however, has been defined and understood in a variety of ways, and before proceeding to discuss specific categories and examples found in NRMs, we will introduce a perspective on myth that we will apply throughout this section. We will then provide instances of the ways in which crucial events in the passage of time, from the creation of the world to its eventual demise in an eschatological future, are presented in various NRMs. We will highlight in particular how the ideology of these movements is reflected in mythological form. As mentioned in the Introduction, religion, as we understand it, can take other shapes than organizations with a well-defined locus of authority, and the last part of this section deals with the ways in which mythological creativity can function when people in loose networks united by little more than an interest in unconventional ideas jointly create stories about the emergence of human civilization or the structure of the cosmos.

Approaching the Study of Myths

The term "myth" is, and has been, understood in a bewildering variety of ways. One common approach is to define it as a particular narrative genre. Consider this bare-bones summary of the story told in the first chapter of the book of Genesis. The narrative explains God's first steps were creating the heavens and the earth. Gradually transforming and setting in order a world of darkness and chaos, God created light, separated land from water, and made vegetation spring forth. God arranged the heavenly bodies, created the innumerable animals that populate the world, and ended the job by creating human beings "in his image." The narrative we just offered, minimalist and lackluster as it may be, fits the definition proposed in a widely cited text that defines myths in terms of their genre (Bascom 1965). It deals with a time in the distant past when the world was being organized and it has a suprahuman protagonist (God) as its main character.

In popular usage, myth often serves to refer to a narrative that does not accurately represent the facts of a situation. This meaning of the word is commonly traced back to the ancient Greeks, and to Plato in particular, who distinguished *mythos* from *logos*. While these two terms have a convoluted history, the latter eventually came to signify a true account as opposed to the far more dubious *mythos*.[2] Adopting the normative evaluation that results from imposing such a dichotomy, proponents of evolutionist and secularist understandings of cultural change assumed that mythological accounts of matters like the origin of the cosmos would give way to scientific ones in modern societies. This, however, has clearly not been the case: old myths are retold, and new ones continue to be created, which demonstrates that such narratives are as central as ever to the religious imagination. Unsurprisingly, stories that we classify as myths continue to be told by many religious insiders simply because from their perspective, they are true. For millions of conservative Christians, for instance, the creation accounts appearing in Genesis remain relevant because from their viewpoint, they are accurate renderings of historical happenings. Approaches that stress that myths fulfill important functions other than merely offering explanations for diverse phenomena suggest additional reasons for their persistence in the modern age. For example, an insistence upon the first human couple having been created separately from all other creatures provides a counternarrative against a Darwinian account that many regard as a sinister attack on Christian core values; for many, this has become a central identity marker for a range of religiously conservative people who may identify their beliefs as creationist.

Functionalist accounts of myth go back to the emergence of the study of religions, but radically divergent opinions have been voiced throughout the history of the field regarding precisely what that function is.[3] Does myth encode fundamental processes in the human psyche, as Sigmund Freud and Carl Jung, each in their own distinct way, maintained? Is it the expression of a profound truth about a sacred reality, as Mircea Eliade proposed? Does it, as Claude Lévi-Strauss suggested, arrange thought in accordance with the rules of an underlying structural grammar? Although Freudian, Jungian, Eliadean, and structuralist approaches continue to have advocates, their influence appears to have waned over time. By contrast, a substantial and enduring stream of writings explores the function that

---

[2] Lincoln (1999: 3–43) discusses the shifting meanings of the two terms in antiquity.

[3] Surveys of various approaches to myth include Strenski (1987), Dubuisson (2014), and Segal (2021). For a brief, but quite inclusive list, see McCutcheon (2000: 193–8).

myths fulfill in legitimizing particular social orders. We find an early example in *Myth in Primitive Psychology* (originally published in 1926) where the anthropologist Bronislaw Malinowski suggests that myths are narratives that justify present-day customs, such as carrying out a ritual or following a social rule, by narrating how those customs stretch back to the dawn of time. Malinowski's approach to myth largely sees a society and its culture as an organic whole that functions smoothly because myths provide the fundamental charter that legitimizes the social order. Any complex society will, however, encompass people with different interests, and later writers have explored the role myths can have in justifying social inequalities and the dominance of one group over others. Roland Barthes' *Mythologies* (1957), in particular, explores the ways in which narratives, rituals, and images can simultaneously convey an overt surface message and project an underlying ideological subtext. His most celebrated example is a picture featured on the cover of the French magazine *Paris-Match* in which a young Black soldier performs a military salute while facing an object outside the frame of the image that the viewer will, based upon the suggested context, likely assume is a French flag. Barthes' claim that the image legitimized colonial oppression by pretending that people who were colonized by France loyally supported the political order of their colonizers may not seem particularly radical today, but his reading was far more subversive at the time. As this case suggests, Barthes cast the net widely and applied the term "myth" to a very diverse set of data. In more recent years, prominent examples of such approaches that focus on the ideological functions of myths in a narrower sense, that is, narratives that form part of a religious system, include Bruce Lincoln (1999) and Russell McCutcheon (2000).

That myths are permeated by ideological messages is hardly a controversial statement. Stories about human origins can argue that wealth ought to be in the hands of certain people and not others, that only a particular social group should wield power, that one gender is inherently superior, or that one ethnic group should be allowed to dominate others. The myth of the Fall told in chapter 3 of Genesis describes the expulsion of the first human couple from the Garden of Eden, an event that forced them to exchange their previously utopian existence for a life in which they would experience suffering. Eve was the first to eat of the famous forbidden fruit, and when God discovered her disobedience, he decreed that all women were henceforth to be ruled over by their husbands (Genesis 3:16). Unsurprisingly, this passage has been frequently invoked to justify patriarchal demarcations of gender roles.

A point that Barthes also makes is that the pervasive underlying ideology his analysis uncovers is that of the dominant class, which for him was the French bourgeoisie. Since NRMs are rarely dominant within their host societies, one would not expect their myths to unequivocally reflect the prevailing ideology of the surrounding culture. On the contrary, the very notion of a minority religion implies that a group of people has concluded that the truths that they proclaim and the practices they espouse are superior to those of the mainstream. This oppositional stance lies at the core of a seeming paradox. New myths are rarely completely novel. Instead, they are constructed through the process of bricolage identified by anthropologist Claude Lévi-Strauss (1966: 16): They are fashioned by people selecting elements from a pool of existing cultural resources, whereby these elements are combined in novel and perhaps unexpected ways, and a few truly innovative claims are added. The myths that place new religions in opposition to the values and beliefs of mainstream society thus depend on the ability of creative individuals to reuse existing cultural elements, and as the following examples illustrate, the oppositional ideological messages they promote will in various ways both reflect and reject some of the values of mainstream society.

Creation Myths

The Nation of Islam, an organization founded in 1930, promotes a message of Black ethno-nationalism crafted in religious terms.[4] A central myth of this movement describes race relations in a distant past. According to it, a Black deity by the name of Allah created the first humans, the tribe of Shabazz, who lived in Mecca and the Nile valley. This first race of human beings was Black, like their creator, and were possessors of an advanced level of scientific knowledge. Roughly 6,000 years ago, one of their most gifted scientists, Yakub, created a new race as the result of a 600-year-long process of breeding. The pale beings that emerged were, however, found to be evil devils. They were dispersed into an area that is today known as Europe and were permitted to rule the world from there for 6,000 years. The myth thus conveys a form of racial gnosis; that is, it teaches the members of the Nation of Islam that Black people and White people are fundamentally different, that White people are inherently inferior, and that the domination of much of the world by people of European descent is coming to an end. In a society that has oppressed and marginalized Black people for centuries, this is clearly an ideologically oppositional counternarrative. At the same time, the myth aligns with key aspects of majority culture. It builds upon and inverts a concept of race that was formulated in the nineteenth century by writers such as Arthur de Gobineau (1816–1882), whose publications present history in racial terms and extol the supposed superiority of Whites. Although early sources sometimes present the myth as an undisputed

---

[4] On the Nation of Islam, see Gardell (1996). Its origin myth is summarized and discussed in Ansari (1981: 162–7).

truth and sometimes as the result of a revelation,[5] it later becomes framed as an account supported by science and hence adopts a mode of legitimation that has become ubiquitous in the contemporary religious landscape (cf. Lewis 2003). The newspaper of the movement, *The Final Call*, published an article in which a collective of authors known as the NOI Research Group describes in rhetorically charged language how evidence provided by "unbiased" scientists "proves" the account.[6] Ultimately, however, references to science function as a way to bolster the authority of the founder of the movement. Secular scientists have, in this version of events, been slow to arrive at a truth that was established eighty years earlier by Elijah Muhammad and which was rendered by him in much greater detail than the accounts modern researchers are able to provide. A narrative about the emergence of distinct human races hence serves as a vehicle for an underlying message that a particular minority perspective is correct, while everybody else has been blind and is only now beginning to see the truth.

One way of classifying new religions is to place them in families of movements with shared historical origins. In his *Encyclopedia of American Religions*, J. Gordon Melton groups various religions together into what he calls families, such as those with roots in the Pentecostal, Baptist, and Adventist traditions, in Judaism, in Zoroastrianism, or in what he calls the Ancient Wisdom families (the latter including movements like Theosophy), to mention just a few. Since many new religions are recent offshoots of historically well-established traditions, they tend to elaborate on the myths of that tradition. A particular movement within such a family can assert that other groups within the same family, as well as the parent organization itself, have misunderstood the sacred texts they have in common and insist that their own understanding is correct. For example, while the Jehovah's Witnesses assert that the world was created by God as stated in Genesis, they reject the label creationists because they interpret the biblical passages in question as telling the story of a very ancient world that was brought into being over a vast stretch of time.[7] There are, however, many varieties of Christian creationism, and not all creationists understand the six days of creation mentioned in the first chapter of Genesis as referring to six consecutive twenty-four-hour units of time. The Jehovah's Witnesses' explicit rejection of any suggestion that they are creationists ought to

---

[5] The summary of the myth that one finds in the founder Elijah Muhammad's *Message to the Blackman* is in part presented as if it were mere fact, but in chapter 29 of his book and elsewhere there are suggestions that it was Allah who revealed the racial truth.

[6] *The Final Call*, May 13, 2013, issue, www.finalcall.com/artman/publish/Perspectives_1/art icle_9878.shtml.

[7] See, e.g., www.jw.org/en/jehovahs-witnesses/faq/creationism-belief/.

be seen, at least in part, as an attempt at branding so as to distinguish themselves from a range of movements they do not regard as being truly (i.e., biblically based) Christian.

The cosmogony of the Mormons (the Church of Jesus Christ of Latter-day Saints, or LDS) is also rooted in biblical mythology but has developed features of its own which convey a distinct ideological message.[8] LDS sources do not focus solely on what one might call the mechanics of creation but also, and even primarily, on the reason, as they see it, why a material universe was fashioned in the first place. Here, the world is portrayed as a stage upon which a cosmic drama – the plan of salvation – plays out. Every human being, from an LDS perspective, has a spiritual component that lived a premortal existence before the world was created. At one point in time, God – commonly referred to as Heavenly Father in LDS terminology – organized a great council in heaven to be attended by all spirits. As part of the proceedings, he presented his plans for creating the cosmos. The actual task itself would be carried out by Jesus, which he did by fashioning everything out of pre-existent matter. The material world was intended to be a place for us to be born as mortal beings and to be tested as such. Since temptation would inevitably lead some individuals astray, a redeemer would therefore be necessary. Two spirits volunteered – Jesus and Lucifer. The latter wished to redeem all of humankind, but this would, of course, mean that no one would have a choice in the matter. Jesus, by contrast, insisted that human beings had free will and could choose to reject the offer of redemption. God therefore selected Jesus for this role. Lucifer rebelled against the decision and was subsequently cast out of heaven. The plan was then set in motion, and a string of significant events thus ensued, with material creation, the fall of Adam and Eve, and the Atonement (Jesus' sacrificial death) being major milestones along the way. Implicit in this story are various moral lessons. In addition to the explicit theme of obedience as a key virtue, we also find the underlying belief that the world is an arena where we are tested, which calls for an answer to the question what one should do and believe in order to pass the test. The *Guide to the Scriptures* published by the LDS Church specifies that salvation entails "obedience to the laws and ordinances of the gospel and service to Christ" and that these in turn include repentance for sins one has committed.[9] The moral preferences formulated by spokespersons of the Church regarding precisely which acts are sinful are in this way placed within a cosmological framework that defines these values as divinely sanctioned. Since the Church

---

[8] Succinct insider accounts of cosmogony and its soteriological importance according to LDS theology can be found in Nielsen & Ricks (1992) and Lund (1992), respectively.

[9] www.churchofjesuschrist.org/study/manual/gospel-topics/salvation?lang=eng.

sees prophetic guidance as active in the present, revelations still to come can change the boundaries between sinful and acceptable values.

Other NRMs utilize even more innovative reworkings of the Jewish and Christian myths in their narratives about such matters as the origin of the cosmos and the creation and fate of the first humans in a distant past. One such example is the case of Raëlianism, a UFO religion founded in the mid-1970s, where the impact of science and technology in the contemporary period has served to shape its reinterpretations of stories found in Genesis. The movement's founder, Claude Vorilhon (b. 1946), later known as Raël, claims that he witnessed a UFO landing and was thereafter approached by a small humanoid creature.[10] Over the next six days, it revealed to him a set of fundamental facts about life, including the true meaning of the biblical story of creation. When understood correctly, Genesis 1 shows how humans were in fact created by technologically advanced extraterrestrials, according to Raël's informant. Elohim, the term for God used in Genesis 1, is actually the name of these highly evolved beings. This is something that existing traditions have misunderstood, Raël writes, due to the cultural level of our ancestors being so low that they could only interpret these genetic engineers from space as gods.

Another space-age myth, one with echoes of science fiction rather than discernible connections to any pre-existing religion, is the story of Xenu that forms part of the mythology of Scientology.[11] The organizational structure of Scientology consists of a number of levels, and the contents of the most advanced stages are kept secret from those who have not yet reached that point in their journey. Most Scientologists never reach the level known as OT-III, where the Xenu myth is revealed to them, and although various retellings of it are easy to find on the Internet, as a normative ideal they will be unaware of the details.[12] To summarize the story briefly, Xenu is the name of the ruler of a Galactic Confederacy who, according to this mythological account, lived seventy-five million years ago and who decided to rid his overpopulated dominions of many of its inhabitants (who in many respects resembled humans of the 1950s and 1960s, i.e., the time when L. Ron Hubbard created Scientology). He did so by having his troops round up citizens in spaceships

---

[10] The purported events are related in his book *Le livre qui dit la vérité* (1974; "The Book that Tells the Truth").

[11] On the Xenu myth, see Rothstein (2009); Lewis (2016).

[12] Although the Church of Scientology has attempted to reserve knowledge of the Xenu myth for members who have reached the highest levels of the movement, it has become widely known after being lampooned in an episode of the animated series South Park ("Trapped in the Closet," season 9, episode 12) and is described in detail in a Wikipedia article, https://en.wikipedia.org/wiki/Xenu, which at the time of this writing is the top result retrieved when doing a Google search for the term Xenu.

that looked like DC-8 airplanes in order to transport them to Earth, then known as Teegeeack, where they were subsequently deposited on large volcanos and then blown up with H-bombs. According to Scientology, individuals are soul-like entities called thetans; although humans also have physical bodies, these merely house the soul or thetan. The thetans of those who had been slaughtered during the cosmic genocide were captured and forced to endure a form of mental torture involving the implantation of false ideas and the loss of a sense of personal identity. Clusters of these so-called body thetans cling to or surround present-day thetans, and high-level Scientologists who have been given access to this esoteric myth attempt to counteract the negative effects said to be caused by these entities.[13] The myth of Xenu thus serves as a justification for a particular ritual practice – namely auditing and self-examination using the e-meter – and also explains why other methods of removing obstacles to living an optimal life, the professed goal of the movement, are insufficient. Beneath its space-age surface, the narrative and its associated practices also tap into a widespread ideological presupposition found in modern Western countries, namely, the notion that problems encountered in life can only be tackled individually rather than collectively. The ultimate aim of Scientology, to "clear the planet," is in this respect a solo project to be undertaken step by step by one individual at a time.

Cosmologies

The myths of more traditional religions and newer ones alike can present highly elaborate descriptions of how the cosmos is built up and the place of humanity within it. Given that each religion is a product of a particular place and time, it follows that they are infused in various ways with the concerns peculiar to a specific cultural context. The mythology of the LDS Church presents the cosmos as being heliocentric and comprising numerous stars and planets; it is thus characteristic of an age when the universe was no longer viewed as a geocentric system of planets surrounded by a sphere of fixed stars. Although heliocentric models were proposed by some thinkers already in ancient Greece, a geocentric view of the cosmos reigned supreme until the work of Copernicus (1473–1543) and Galileo (1564–1642) provided the arguments that would ultimately lead to an astronomical paradigm shift. In the texts of the LDS Church, we find a cosmology that arose in the intellectual culture of early modern Europe and had become mainstream in the nineteenth century projected back unto ancient biblical times. The Book of Mormon itself, a volume

---

[13] A far more detailed explanation of the role of body thetans in the world view of Scientology can be found in Bromley (2009: 90–6).

comprising what are said to be historical records documenting the lives and spiritual fates of people who purportedly lived in the Americas in pre-Columbian times, only mentions such themes in passing, but the reader is informed that "surely it is the earth that moveth and not the sun" (Helaman 12:15).

One of the other key texts of the LDS Church, the Book of Abraham,[14] contains a more extensive narrative that, while not always easy to interpret, clearly posits the existence of a vast cosmos with many heavenly bodies. The text itself, which is fairly short and consists of five chapters, is based on what Joseph Smith described as a translation of an Egyptian text written on several papyrus sheets.[15] In the third chapter of the Book of Abraham, the patriarch is granted a vision of the origin and structure of the cosmos with the aid of the Urim and Thummim, a divinely crafted prophetic instrument made up of two stones fashioned into a pair of spectacles. What Abraham is led to understand is that various heavenly bodies are placed at varying distances from the throne of God, the closest being Kolob, a star which rather mysteriously is said "to govern all those planets which belong to the same order as that upon which thou [i.e., Abraham] standest."[16] He also learns that time passes differently on different planets and stars, the "highest" of these heavenly bodies having the slowest "reckoning of time," but the density and obscurity of the source text, Abraham 3: 6–9, makes it difficult to unpack the details:

> **6** [–] it is given unto thee to know the times of reckoning, and the set time, yea, the set time of the earth upon which thou standest, and the set time of the greater light which is set to rule the day, and the set time of the lesser light which is set to rule the night.
>
> **7** Now the set time of the lesser light is a longer time as to its reckoning than the reckoning of the time of the earth upon which thou standest.
>
> **8** And where these two facts exist, there shall be another fact above them, that is, there shall be another planet whose reckoning of time shall be longer still;
>
> **9** And thus there shall be the reckoning of the time of one planet above another, until thou come nigh unto Kolob, which Kolob is after the reckoning of the Lord's time; which Kolob is set nigh unto the throne of God, to govern all those planets which belong to the same order as that upon which thou standest.

---

[14] The Book of Abraham is included in the Pearl of Great Price, a canonical scripture of the LDS Church.

[15] According to Joseph Smith, the papyri contained a text written by the biblical patriarch Abraham, whereas Egyptologists have identified it as an example of an Egyptian funerary text, the *Book of Breathings*. Unsurprisingly, these incommensurable assessments of the text have inspired a range of apologetic and debunking responses. For a detailed review of the issues, see Vogel (2021).

[16] One can note that an article on scriptural references to astronomy in the *Encyclopedia of Mormonism*, a work compiled by LDS insiders, also treats the discussions of Kolob as "not clear" (Paul 1992). See also Athay (1968).

In addition to the smattering of references found in these two texts, the reader of Doctrine and Covenants, a set of revelations given to Joseph Smith also considered scripture by the LDS Church, will find a passage stating that there is life on numerous other planets (D&C 76: 24) and that the beings that inhabit these celestial bodies are "begotten sons and daughters unto God," but the ultimate focus of LDS mythology is our own world.

Historiographical Myths and Endtime Scenarios

Besides recounting stories about a distant past when the world as we know it came into existence, many religions, traditional as well as new, have narratives that present the course of history as adhering to an overarching model. For instance, one widespread Protestant perspective sees history as a series of dispensations, whereas a common Hindu understanding is that a Golden Age has been followed by a series of further periods characterized by decline. Many religions, especially those that are historically rooted in Jewish and Christian traditions, also have stories about the Endtimes. As is also the case with their origin myths, a familiarity with the conceptions of history and the future found in the parent tradition is crucial to understanding the narratives of each individual NRM.

The International Society for Krishna Consciousness, or ISKCON, has borrowed from its predecessors in India, and more specifically from descriptions found in the Bhagavata Purana (a text that ISKCON sources refer to as the Śrīmad Bhagavatam), the idea that we are presently living in the worst of all ages, *kali yuga*. Current events and social mores can be regarded through the lens of Puranic passages such as this:

> Religion, truthfulness, cleanliness, tolerance, mercy, duration of life, physical strength and memory will all diminish day by day because of the powerful influence of the age of Kali. Srimad Bhagavatam 12.2.1 (Translation by A. C. Bhaktivedanta Swami Prabhupada)

It requires little effort to find evidence of the existence of some of the elements appearing on the list of evils characterizing kali yuga in our present times.[17] Secularism, some would say, is rampant, and a general lack of tolerance and mercy in the world today can be seen as the root cause of the innumerable conflicts that seem to be raging at any given moment. While it might, in light of advances that have been made in medical science, seem counterintuitive to posit that lifespans have become shorter, such progress, seen from an ISKCON perspective, is minor and limited since kali yuga, according to this particular

---

[17] See, e.g., https://krishna.org/kali-yuga-the-problems-and-the-solution/.

view of history, was preceded by far superior ages when lives were considerably longer. During *dvapara yuga*, the second-worst age and the one that directly preceded kali yuga, people lived for roughly 1,000 years, a number that is dwarfed in comparison with the lifespans of 100,000 years that are said to have been the norm during *satya yuga*, the best of all ages. The Golden Age motif we see here serves to legitimize the practices of the ISKCON movement: since we live in a degenerate age and have severely limited capabilities, the only realistic spiritual path available to us is to devote our lives to serving Krishna.

In addition to regarding history as a process that unfolds according to an overarching plan, many religions, both old and new, offer mythological accounts of what the future will hold and how it all will end. What unites these very diverse forms of millennialism, simply put, is the notion that the future, regardless of whether the events described are to take place in this world or in a radically different dimension, will offer far better conditions than the ones existing at present – at least for those who have chosen the right religion. In the Western world, millennialism has traditionally been based on the in some respects quite cryptic Endtime scenario of the New Testament Book of Revelation as well as various passages scattered throughout the Bible that lend themselves to being combined and read in such a way so as to provide information about things to come. Due not least to the influence of popular culture, one way of interpreting the eschaton, dispensationalism, is at least minimally familiar to a wide audience. This particular view is rooted in the idea that supernatural intervention will soon disrupt the course of history and that various events leading up to the end of things as we know them, such as the Rapture, the rule of the Antichrist, and the battle of Armageddon, have been foretold in the Bible (for details, see the discussion in Section 4 on the creative reuse of texts).

The basic elements of this millennialist message can also be reinterpreted and subsequently used by NRMs that at a first glance may appear to be far removed from the Christian family of religions. The Heaven's Gate movement, for example, notorious for the mass suicide of thirty-nine of its members in 1997, might seem like an exotic cacophony of ufology, beliefs from the New Age scene, and the rather idiosyncratic ideas of its founders, but the key role of dispensationalism has been noted by scholars such as Benjamin E. Zeller (2014: 106–12). To take but one example, there is a passage in the Book of Revelation (11:3–13) that speaks of "two witnesses" who at the end of time will prophesy for 1,290 days before being killed by "the Beast." Three and a half days later, they will come back to life and ascend to heaven in a cloud. The leaders of Heaven's Gate, Marshall Applewhite (1931–1997) and Bonnie Nettles (1927–1985), interpreted this passage as referring to themselves, and they understood the part about a journey to heaven as involving a spaceship. The dispensationalist concept of the Rapture relies upon a passage in Paul's First Epistle to the Thessalonians (4:17), according to which the righteous, both among the living and dead, will at the time in question rise up in the air and meet Jesus. This, too, was interpreted by Applewhite and Nettles in ufological terms as amounting to a promise that those who heeded their message would be picked up in bodily form by a UFO that would take them to the next evolutionary level. However, after Nettles passed away, this understanding changed dramatically. According to the new reading, Heaven's Gate members would, instead of being transported by a spaceship, need to shed their physical bodies in order to transition to what they called TELAH – The Evolutionary Level Above Human. Ultimately, this reinterpretation of the Rapture served to justify the actions of those adherents who chose to take their own lives.

Myths in Cultic Milieus

The myths we have presented so far are the brainchildren of the founders and leaders of structured social movements, but cosmological speculation as well as stories about the distant past or the Endtimes also circulate in the cultic milieu. Here, myths can be created by authors of books that will be widely disseminated, or they may be constructed through processes of negotiation involving larger groups of people with little or no discernible hierarchical structure in place that would allow any one person to impose their own narrative in top-down fashion. Such narratives may have features that situate them in an indeterminate space between the secular and the religious. One example is myths that tell of the origins of various fundamental elements of human culture in the distant past. Two well-known cases from ancient mytho-logical traditions are, first, the story of Prometheus as the heroic figure who brought fire from the realm of the gods to humanity; and, second, the account found in Genesis 4: 4–5 that relates how the institution of animal sacrifice had its origin in the deity's acceptance of Abel's sacrifice. Modern counterparts also give credit for major cultural advances to ancient encounters with myth-ical creatures, but rather than presenting these beings as divine, they are in some instances described as emissaries from a technically and spiritually advanced Ice Age civilization and in others as humanoid visitors from outer space that our ancestors mistook as gods. The former theme – that a lost civilization introduced cultural innovations to various hunter-gatherer popu-lations – has been promoted by the immensely successful British author and media personality Graham Hancock (b. 1950). Swiss hotelier and author Erich von Däniken (b. 1935) gained celebrity status when his book *Chariots of the*

Gods (1968) popularized the latter idea, that is, that aliens had kick-started significant cultural developments around the globe. Although both of these now ubiquitous motifs are associated with well-known individuals, they are the results of an ongoing process of bricolage carried out by a range of authors combining narrative elements that in some cases can be traced back to the nineteenth century (cf. Hammer & Swartz 2021, 2024).

The idea that things were better in the past is a sentiment that resonates with many people and is commonplace outside the context of NRMs as well. Romanticized notions of the splendors of life in a preindustrial society inform such popular motifs as the noble savage, which is frequently encountered in various cultural products such as Kevin Costner's hugely successful film *Dances with Wolves* (1990). In the twenty-first century, a new mythological version of the motif of a Golden Age followed by a period of cultural decline has emerged as an Internet phenomenon with distinct conspiratorial undertones promoted by both a small number of active YouTubers and a much larger group of people who together negotiate the contours and meaning of this nascent narrative. The basic storyline goes something like this: The view of history promoted by the cultural mainstream is in essence a complete fabrication crafted by a shadowy elite in an attempt to erase all traces of a glorious earlier civilization, the Tartarian Empire, which once ruled the world. The evidence for its great achievements can nonetheless be found all around us by those who have been awakened to the truth. Lavish buildings dating from a time prior to the rapid spread of modernist architecture are seen within the framework of this conspiracy-tinged mythology as just such traces. Some versions of the Tartarian Empire tale suggest that certain details, like lightning rods or spires, are actually the remains of Tartarian technological devices that could gather energy from the ethers. This, the story goes, is one of the reasons why the elite want to dupe us into believing a fake version of history: simply put, Tartarian technology would undermine the monopoly of the petrochemical industry.

In addition to their scientific savvy, the Tartarians were also spiritually superior. One claim asserts that Tartarian culture was "based on unity, oneness, peace, love, and harmony, which we don't see in today's society."[18] Much of the architecture attributed to the Tartarians is built on a grand scale, with ceilings soaring high above the heads of visitors. A frequently encountered explanation for this choice is that the Tartarians, or at least a number of them, were giants, beings possibly connected to the mysterious Nephilim mentioned in Genesis

---

[18] From an interview with Tartarian Empire theory supporter Joachim Skaar, cited in www .bloomberg.com/news/features/2021-04-27/inside-architecture-s-wildest-conspiracy-theory.

6:4. Different views abound when it comes to the matter of what caused the Tartarian Empire to disappear, with one explanation attributing it to a cataclysmic mudslide. An abundance of ideas, which are combined in various creative ways, thus flourishes on social media platforms like YouTube and Facebook. These are spaces where they are reworked anew as people comment upon postings and fresh elements are added. In terms of structure, much of this mythology resembles accounts also found in more traditional myths, like the story told in the first chapters of Genesis: a people that mastered such skills as city planning (Genesis 4:17) and metalworking (4:22) lived at a time when giants populated the Earth (6:4) but were wiped out by a global flood (Genesis 6:5 to chapter 8). The Tartarian complex of myths retains this basic skeletal narrative, except, here, the Tartarians are the good guys who are wiped out by the ancestors of the people who currently dominate the Earth, rather than the wicked ones who are annihilated by a cataclysm.

Like their more structured counterparts, cultic milieus can also encompass myths about the unfolding of history and millennial aspirations.[19] During the 1960s and 1970s, and also to a lesser extent in subsequent decades, the idea that the passage of time comprises a succession of astrological ages flourished. The belief that the Age of Pisces, which according to this understanding of history was characterized by the predominance of Christianity, was transitioning into the Age of Aquarius, a period that would usher in an evolutionary leap in human consciousness, was a widespread one. The concept of astrological ages is based on the phenomenon of axial precession, that is, a gradual shift in the way the rotational axis of the Earth is oriented. For an observer looking at the sky from the vantage point of our planet, the slow movement of the axis makes the apparent position of the sun relative to the backdrop of the stars seem to travel very slowly through the zodiac. The idea that transitions from one sign to the next are in some way connected to major cultural changes was most notably expressed by Theosophical writers such as Alice Bailey (1880–1949). In her book *The Destiny of the Nations* (1949), for instance, we find a chapter entitled "Initiation in the Aquarian Age." It was also the opening number of the musical *Hair* (1967), in which references to astrological lore are encapsulated in lyrics like "peace will guide the planets and love will steer the stars," that introduced it to a much wider audience. The generally utopian-hued understanding of what the Age of Aquarius would be like entered New Age discourse in the 1970s, and Marilyn Ferguson's book *The Aquarian Conspiracy* (1980) placed the idea that the emergence of new forms of spirituality signified a shift in human consciousness firmly on the cultural map. There was, however, as Lucas (2011) notes,

---

[19] On this topic, see also several of the contributions in Harvey & Newcombe (2013).

widespread disagreement in this particular milieu, due to its fuzzy contours and lack of central authority, about precisely when this transition was to happen. In addition to numerous optimistic renditions of this millennialistic myth, there were also voices that spoke of a considerably darker time to come. Those who drew on the prophetic utterances of Edgar Cayce, for example, could imagine the road ahead as one sign transitioned to the next as marked by catastrophic geological change (Lucas 2011: 581–4). Extensive divergences in opinion resurfaced a few decades later as another millennial myth was negotiated, this time in connection with discussions regarding the so-called 2012 phenomenon. The belief that the Mayan calendar would come to an end on December 21 of that year, an event that would have momentous consequences for the entire world, inspired a spectrum of views ranging from optimistic ideas about collective spiritual advancement for all of humanity to dire warnings about impending global disaster (Hoopes 2011).

Finally, besides being present in both older and more recently founded religious movements, cosmologies that depart from those espoused by the cultural mainstream can also be found in the cultic milieu. We conclude this section by presenting a cosmology that departs radically from the consensus view: Flat Earth theory. Like the Tartarian myth, it is largely a bricolage constructed within a network of interested individuals who may be more or less passive and a smaller number of highly active proponents. It has been widely understood since the days of ancient Greece that the Earth is roughly spherical, and Flat Earth theory of the kind discussed here is not a reflection of a premodern cosmological concept but a modern movement which originated in the mid-nineteenth century. Its roots can be traced to the work of Samuel Birley Rowbotham (1816–1884), who published three successive and increasingly elaborate versions of a text entitled *Zetetic Astronomy: Earth Not a Globe*, under the pseudonym Parallax. The first version, which appeared in 1846, consists of a mere sixteen pages. The third version, published in 1881 and the one cited here, is a substantial volume of 430 pages. In modern Flat Earth theories, we find the core elements of his cosmology reproduced, such as envisioning the Earth as a flat disc encircled by a wall of ice over which the sun and moon, two relatively small objects, move at a distance of no more than a few thousand miles (Rowbotham 1881: 353–4). Rowbotham devotes a sizeable portion of the book to recounting observations and experiments that he insists support his views and refuting arguments suggesting that the Earth is a sphere. In the book's fourteenth chapter, highly detailed religious reasoning enters the picture as he affirms the absolute authority of the Bible in this matter and endorses a view of history that considers the Earth to be roughly 6,000 years old. Various passages in the Bible, Rowbotham argues, affirm that the Earth is flat and that the sun moves across it; he therefore denounces a cosmology depicting the Earth as a sphere as "a prolific source of irreligion and of atheism, of which its advocates are practically supporters … [by] defending a system which is directly opposed to that which is taught in connection with the Jewish and Christian religion" (Rowbotham 1881: 354). Tracing the many twists and turns of the path leading from such early exponents of Flat Earth theory to today's largely Internet-based pockets of belief goes, however, beyond the confines of this Element.[20]

The examples of myths that have emerged in cultic milieus illustrate with particular clarity one of the main points of this section, namely the way in which even the most vigorous opposition to various values and beliefs that are prevalent in mainstream society is constructed by drawing upon familiar tropes. Even such minority narratives as the Tartarian myth and Flat Earth cosmology that have been debunked and ridiculed by outsiders build upon such well-known motifs as nostalgia for a golden age, distrust of the institutional pillars of society, and an individualistic ethos that insists that facts are immediately available to common sense. These underlying motifs are so pervasive in contemporary Western societies that the 2022 Netflix series *Ancient Apocalypse*, featuring Graham Hancock's narrative of a glorious culture-bearing Ice Age civilization that has left traces in the archaeological evidence that are readily apparent to unbiased investigators such as Hancock himself but invisible to or actively denied by the "archaeological orthodoxy," became one of the company's most widely streamed productions.

2 Rituals

People perform a wide range of actions as part of their allegiance to a religious tradition: they fast, pray, go on pilgrimages, dance, sing, consult diviners, attend communal acts of worship, celebrate key moments of the year, initiate young members of the community into the adult world, and carry out numerous other activities in ways that are in one sense or another connected to their concepts of a suprahuman dimension. In brief: they carry out rituals. If, as anthropologist Roy Rappaport suggested, rituals are "the social act basic to humanity" (1999: 31), it follows that rituals are ubiquitous and would be an essential part of emergent contemporary religions as well, a fact that will be amply illustrated in this section.

The reference to a suprahuman dimension in our description of what rituals are has the advantage of separating out religious rituals from other kinds of culturally prescribed, set ways of behaving (e.g., a handshake could be seen as

---

[20] This history has been documented in depth in Garwood (2007).

a nonreligious ritual). Although the present section focuses squarely on religious rituals, we will in Section 5 briefly return to the fact that such rituals are nevertheless often closely related to other cultural behaviors. Ritual purification and the ordinary washing of hands in order to maintain hygiene build on similar cognitively hardwired impulses to avoid contagion (see Section 5 of this Element), but only the former would qualify as ritual under any definition commonly encountered in the study of religion. Talking to another person and addressing a personal prayer to a deity can activate similar social and cognitive mechanisms (Schjødt et al. 2009), and again, only one of these activities would normally be called a ritual.

Although rituals have been of interest to people engaged in the study of religions since the field's earliest days, no generally agreed-upon definition of what the term "ritual" actually means has ever been formulated, nor has any taxonomy ever been constructed that has managed to gain general acceptance within the scholarly community (see, e.g., Grimes 2000 and Bell 2009b: 69–70 for an overview of the definitional problems). One of the most influential theorists of ritual studies, Catherine Bell (2009a: 91), notes that some categories have nevertheless become common reference points in much of the literature. Her heuristic classification includes six "fairly standard ritual genres": rites of passage; seasonal and commemorative rites; rites of exchange and communion; rites of affliction; rites of feasting, fasting, and festivals; and political rituals. What follows are brief illustrations of these categories, with an emphasis on the first four.

Rites of Passage

One classic area of study concerns rites of passage, rituals that mark the transition from one station in life to another. A model originally formulated by Arnold van Gennep (1873–1957) in his book *The Rites of Passage* (first published in 1909 as *Les rites de passage*) and later refined and extended by anthropologist Victor Turner (1920–1983), divides such rituals into three stages. The individual undergoing the ritual is first separated from the social group to which they belong. During the liminal stage, the individual is seen as being malleable: no longer belonging to the old group, they are ready to be transformed – often by symbolic means – into a member of a new group. Finally, in the third phase, the person re-enters society, now with a new social role or status. Of particular interest for our present purposes are initiatory societies, all of which will have rituals that serve to move members from one level to the next within the organization. Typically, such multilevel religious movements will, at least in theory, try to regulate the information made available to an individual depending upon the level they have reached.

For example, members of the Ordo Templi Orientis (OTO) are provided with an opportunity to participate in a number of symbolic dramas through which they can gradually ascend from the lowest tier up through a hierarchy of various degrees. The precise contents of each step are kept secret, and it is expected that initiates not reveal the details to outsiders or others moving up the ranks. The Church of Scientology offers a somewhat different initiatory path. In this case reaching the highest levels within its organizational structure means gaining access to texts and techniques not made available to those on a lower rung. For example, the Xenu myth briefly discussed in the preceding section is only shared with the minority of members who reach one of these higher levels. The Transcendental Meditation movement also consists of a number of levels, and entry-level initiation involves receiving a personal mantra not to be disclosed to others.

As these examples suggest, the emphasis on secrecy found in movements having little or no direct historical connection to each other indicates that this is a common element in how religions in general and NRMs in particular can be constructed. In addition, it is clear that secrets fulfill a basic social function. Georg Simmel (1858–1918), one of the founding scholars of sociology, noted in his classic essay on secrecy that one of the key functions of keeping some information confidential is that it lets others know that such secrets exist (Simmel, 1992: 421–2). Secret knowledge not only defines a group of people who are privy to it – initiates with privileged insight – but also defines an out-group that has not undergone a particular rite of passage and hence lacks this knowledge, and thus draws a boundary between the two. The existence of secrets and the concomitant unequal control over such scarce resources as privileged information is closely linked to the ability of centrally placed people in the in-group to wield authority over other members of the organization and to mobilize material resources (Urban 2021). Some organizations enjoy financial benefits based on the atmosphere of secrecy maintained. Ascending to the highest levels of Scientology, for instance, is a costly affair. If every interested individual were made privy to the information which now is at least in theory to be transmitted only to those who reach the top, the organization would subsequently lose a significant source of income. Learning how to use a mantra with the technique taught within the Transcendental Meditation movement also involves paying a fee, albeit a far more modest one. According to disgruntled ex-members and other critics, the supposedly secret mantra imparted during the ritual can be determined from a simple table where the gender and age of the initiate are the determining factors.[21] Here, too, making such information – in this case, meditation instructions and a list of mantras – available to the general public would cause the organization to take a major financial hit.

---

[21] See, e.g., the list of mantras posted on http://minet.org/mantras.html.

Seasonal Rituals

Whereas rites of passage structure the flow of time in people's lives as a series of stages, calendrical rituals mark the movement of time more generally in culturally meaningful terms. Bell identifies two subcategories of calendrical rituals – seasonal rituals (addressed here) and commemorative rituals (addressed subsequently). These moments in time are either particularly significant according to the calendar used within a culture or represent important phases in the turning of the seasons.

A minority religion can impose order on time by relying upon or reusing existing traditions prevalent in the larger cultural context in which they are embedded or, alternatively, by creating entirely new occasions to be ritually observed. The latter option can serve to help an NRM construct an identity of its own that distinguishes it from the cultural mainstream. Many Pagans celebrate the solstices, equinoxes, and midpoints (roughly) between them and thus follow a distinct festival calendar. Ronald Hutton (2008) has demonstrated how this way of celebrating the yearly cycle is a modern construction which can be traced to writers from the mid-eighteenth to the mid-twentieth centuries who imaginatively reinterpreted or simply invented pre-Christian religious traditions from the Celtic world and continental Europe. Influential representatives of the Celtic revival, such as Iolo Morganwg (Edward Williams, 1747–1826), connected the celebration of the solstices and equinoxes to the ancient Druids while British archaeologist Margaret Murray (1863–1963), some generations later, claimed that the observance of the beginning of the seasons, roughly half-way been the solstices and equinoxes, was part of an ancient European religion that had managed to survive despite intense repression by various Churches. By the early 1950s, all eight festivals were being celebrated by Wiccans, members of the earliest and thus prototypical Pagan movement. Since then, the custom has spread to other such groups around the globe.

A focus of much anthropological interest has been the ways in which people in premodern societies infuse the basic need for food with rituals. Since the passage of time is generally marked by such groups in terms of a succession of events in the natural world, such rituals can best be seen as seasonal. Hunter-gatherers, for example, may perform rituals in order to ensure success in their hunting endeavors – but typically not in connection with collecting edible wild plants – while groups that reply upon horticulture for their main source of food can ritualize every aspect of the growth cycle of their crops. In modern societies, this connection between acquiring food and performing rituals is far less prevalent. Whereas it remains common in some religious milieus to offer food to a deity or to express gratitude to the powers that be for one's daily sustenance, the production and acquisition of food are, relatively speaking, rarely spiritualized: neither industrial-scale farming nor shopping for groceries is generally associated with religious concepts. Some NRMs, on the other hand, have constructed rituals around such activities as small-scale farming and horticulture, the most elaborate perhaps being biodynamic farming, the ritualized form of crop production implemented by people inspired by Anthroposophy.[22]

At a first glance, biodynamic methods can seem like a version of organic farming. Both shun pesticides, use organic fertilizers, and rely on carefully controlled methods of crop rotation and diversification. Biodynamic production's distinctiveness, however, lies in its use of several ritually prepared substances believed to transmit vital forces to the earth and its reliance on astrological cues for planning the various stages of the farming cycle. One of these substances is made by filling the horn of a cow with manure and leaving it buried in the ground throughout the winter. A second one is made by filling a cow horn with powdered quartz, burying it, and letting it stay underground throughout the summer. The use of this particular receptacle for such preparations is linked to statements made by Rudolf Steiner (1861–1925), the founder of Anthroposophy, about how cows receive streams of etheric and astral formative forces through their horns. Once dug up at the appropriate time, each substance is diluted to extremely low concentrations and processed according to a carefully prescribed method which allows these forces to be mixed thoroughly into the solution before it is finally sprayed over the fields.

Commemorative Rituals

Commemorative rituals, like various seasonal festivals, serve as important identity markers. They celebrate significant moments in the life of a founder of a religious movement, such as their birth, death, or the occasion upon which they attained enlightenment. Rituals of this kind are ubiquitous in NRMs, and for purposes of illustration, we can take an example from Eckankar, a religion founded in 1965 by Paul Twitchell (1908–1971), whose death – or, as ECKists see it, the day he left his physical body – is commemorated on September 17 as Founder's Day. Another such observance, the spiritual new year, falls on October 22, the date upon which the Temple of ECK, its current headquarters in Chanhassen, Minnesota, was consecrated. The Church of Scientology, to cite another example, also celebrates various days seen as having been particularly significant for the establishment of the organization, such as the birthday of L. Ron Hubbard (March 13, 1911). On this occasion, thousands of Scientologists convene at the movement's headquarters in Clearwater, Florida,

---

[22] On biodynamic methods, see Zander (2007: 1579–1607).

to hear inspirational lectures about him. Another significant date is May 9, the date of the initial publication in 1950 of *Dianetics: The Modern Science of Mental Health*. Some movements, like Eckankar and Scientology, focus their attention on one particular individual – the founder. Others, like ISKCON, not only celebrate significant events in the life of their founder A. C. Bhaktivedanta Swami Prabhupada (1896–1977) but also venerate a long lineage of earlier spiritual figures. Some are teachers in a line of gurus and disciples going back to the fifteenth century, while others are incarnations of Krishna that an outsider would likely view as the stuff of myth. The ritual calendar therefore includes such events as a festival in March marking the birth of Chaitanya Mahaprabhu, the founder of the devotional tradition to which ISKCON as one of its present-day representatives belongs, along with days that commemorate the appearances of Krishna's various incarnations, such as the boar Varahadeva in February and as the half-lion, half-man figure of Narasimha in May.

Rites of Exchange and Communion

Typical rites of exchange and communion present offerings to a deity, or deities, for various purposes, ranging from worship to expressing gratitude to seeking a particular reward for having carried out the ritual itself. Movements belonging to the Hindu family of traditions are characterized by frequent performances of rituals of this kind. Whether done in the home, at the workplace, or in temples, rituals present numerous opportunities in which items like fruit, flowers, and incense are offered. Some place a similar emphasis on ritual interaction with a god or goddess. ISKCON again can serve as a case in point. As the representation of Krishna installed in a temple is considered to be in no essential way different from the deity himself, ritual interaction with it is thus perceived as being an actual exchange with the divine, with encounters often prefaced by elaborate procedures of purification and regulated by detailed rules of etiquette. The devotee who is to perform a morning ritual of devotion will first make their presence known by a signal such as ringing a bell before entering the room where the deity resides. In addition to being woken from a night's slumber, the representation will also be offered refreshments at various points throughout the day precisely as any highly esteemed guest would be (Burt 2023: 14–19).

Rituals of Affliction

Rituals of affliction address the multitude of ways in which misfortune can befall an individual. The modern West offers many ritualized ways of dealing with personal tragedy or troubles, whether it be disease, death, conflict, financial problems, or some other form of difficulty, and has an especially broad range of such practices aimed at maintaining and restoring health. In very general terms, we might say that three types of healthcare coexist in these societies. First, there is what we could call institutionalized, biomedical healthcare. This is the system that provides treatment, either following a consultation or after being admitted to the hospital as a patient, based on an evaluation by a medical doctor. Second, there is a regimen of self-care that many of us devise, implement, and attempt to follow in order to prevent problems or cure them if they arise. Taking supplements, staying home from work to recover when ill, and introducing dietary changes are common elements of such programs. Finally, there are ritual modes of healing involving the expertise of people who usually, but not always, operate outside of the official healthcare system, such as acupuncturists, Reiki healers, crystal therapists, reflexologists, and practitioners of homeopathy or Ayurvedic medicine, to name but a few. Individuals trained in these methods would most likely not see their activities as constituting rituals, but from the perspective of the study of religions, it is certainly possible to do so as evidenced by the title of an early, seminal study of such forms of alternative healing practices – *Ritual Healing in Suburban America* (McGuire 1988).

Much of the scientific literature on complementary and alternative medicine (CAM) has as its purpose to evaluate the efficacy of such treatments as medical interventions and the vast majority of this corpus of work is utterly dismissive of most, though not all, of them. At best, these studies typically conclude, they work no better than placebos, and, at worst, they can cause direct harm. Nonetheless, practitioners may attract numerous clients who for various reasons choose to seek out alternatives to conventional healthcare despite the skepticism and who, we have no reason to doubt, feel benefited by the treatments they receive. People suffering from conditions that the biomedical system is ill equipped to address – from chronic fatigue syndrome to the debilitating effects of long COVID – may seek help from CAM practitioners. Others might do so because their affliction can be understood for our purposes here in terms of the distinction commonly drawn in the anthropological literature between illness and disease, the latter covering the gamut of biomedically detectible abnormal conditions and the former referring to a person's experience of feeling unwell. Illness is typically linked to one's cultural context. For example, in many cultures, although no such condition is recognized as a disease by biomedicine, being possessed by a spirit may be a common illness. Similarly, in a Western context, electromagnetic hypersensitivity is not a biomedically recognized diagnosis but can be used by people as a term that subsumes a range of very real, unpleasant symptoms. CAM can address illness in a Western context by offering hope and healing to people suffering from ailments that are either not recognized or deemed untreatable by the biomedical system.

CAM is an umbrella term covering a highly diverse range of interventions, but what many of them share is a number of basic, culturally postulated ideas about what causes one to become ill and how to restore health. These notions can differ radically from biomedical models of disease and treatment. Many forms of CAM presuppose a form of vitalism where health is perceived as being dependent upon a kind of lifeforce referred to by practitioners in various ways, for example, by calling it *energy* or using the Chinese term *qi*. A healthy body is often seen as existing in a state of equilibrium and therefore different illnesses can be attributed to imbalances. Holism implies the idea that bodily, psychological, and social problems may be related and that symptoms affecting one part of the body can be addressed by treating another. In addition to having features recognized by biomedicine, and depending on the form of CAM in question, the body may be understood as also being made up of a number of normally invisible components, such as an aura, nodes of energy referred to as chakras, or conduits of the lifeforce often referred to as meridians, all of which are conceptualized in different and sometimes quite contradictory ways. Attempts to improve health may involve the use of techniques believed to restore balance by channeling life energy into the body or by redirecting it – interventions seen from an insider's point of view as instrumental, effective procedures. Clients who seek out the services of a CAM practitioner frequently report experiencing improvements in their condition after being treated, and this may lead them to conclude that the method works and that the ideas upon which it is based are correct. One way of understanding the somewhat puzzling fact that vastly different sets of underlying assumptions and practices seem to have similar beneficial effects is by viewing the client's session with the CAM practitioner as a ritual in which a number of factors, such as being taken seriously by someone one trusts and having meaning bestowed upon one's ailment, contribute to creating a positive outcome.

The case of Reiki healing can serve to demonstrate why it makes sense to discuss complementary and alternative therapies in a book about NRMs. Like a number of practices that fall into this category, it presupposes the existence of a kind of universal life energy that practitioners can make flow into the body by placing their palms on or above the skin of their patients and may remind an outside observer of other forms of the laying on of hands, such as those performed in charismatic Christian churches. The ability to direct this energy is said to be gained via what are called attunements – rituals that both cleanse and open up aspirants to the Reiki energy. While the details of these events are in an ideal sense to be kept secret, the Internet has made doing so practically impossible.

A ritual such as a Reiki session provides a setting for an individual to have their problems addressed and experiences endowed with meaning.[23] The healer might open the session by asking the client about their situation, giving them time enough to talk about their physical ailments and life circumstances in general. In basic terms, the Reiki ritual itself consists of the practitioner placing their hands either on the body of the client or just above the surface of the skin, often starting at the head and working their way down the body. Although the person on the receiving end of the treatment may only have the faintest idea of what the elusive healing energies actually are, the hand gestures and bodily movements that comprise the ritual provide a visual counterpart of the minimal underlying belief that such energies do exist, and that the practitioner is able to work with them in a way that can prove to be beneficial. Narratives about what one can expect during a session may note entering a state of deep relaxation, changes in body temperature, and experiencing mental images while the eyes are closed. Reading or hearing about such sensations can prime clients to interpret their own experiences during the ritual as signs of efficacy; in other words, the energies are doing what they are supposed to do. The setting itself also reinforces the impression that healing is taking place. From prominently displayed diplomas from various courses to instantly recognizable New Age paraphernalia like rose quartz crystals and Buddha figurines, these and any number of other similar cues add to the feeling of being taken care of and can boost the client's response to the treatment.

Rites of Feasting, Fasting, and Festivals

Rites of feasting, fasting, and festivals are very common in more traditional religions where we find many examples of the ritualized consumption of food or drink, such as Passover seders, communal *langar* meals in the Sikh tradition, or celebrating with sweets to mark the end of Ramadan. Eating together is such an integral part of many cultures that sharing food is also included as an element in religious rituals where the focus lies on something other than refreshments. The elaborate rituals that welcome newcomers to various initiatory societies are not infrequently followed by a shared meal. When Jehovah's Witnesses gather for conventions, large crowds need to be fed, and this was previously done communally.[24] The extent to which religious interpretations are bestowed upon such meals will, however, vary. When members of an organization or movement get together for an event, they will obviously need to eat at some point, and some groups are more prone than others to imbuing the act of dining

---

[23] For an extended discussion of the meaning response, see Moerman (2002).

[24] www.jw.org/en/library/magazines/w20150515/convention-cafeteria-love/.

together with a significance that extends beyond nutritional. Religions having historical and ideological links to a larger tradition where feasting is part of a ritual calendar can build on this heritage and adapt it to the needs of a new religious movement in a contemporary setting. ISKCON can serve as an illuminating example here. There are numerous Indian versions of the ritual of offering food to various deities and the subsequent distribution of it among the attendant worshipers. ISKCON places itself in this tradition by having a particularly elaborate set of concepts underpinning the sharing of food – at least for an NRM. Dishes that are lovingly prepared from religiously acceptable ingredients and ritually offered to Krishna prior to being consumed are referred to as *prasadam*, a Sanskrit word that ISKCON sources translate as "mercy."[25] The positive effects of eating *prasadam* are thought to extend to all regardless of religious affiliation, and thus the Sunday feasts held at many ISKCON temples to which outsiders are welcome are not only opportunities for presenting the movement to nonmembers but also occasions upon which visitors receive the many benefits of eating sanctified food.

Fasting rituals in NRMs with links to older and larger traditions can also be similar modifications of an earlier practice. Fasting, unsurprisingly, is an important part of the ritual calendar of the Nation of Islam, but the link to its mother tradition is far from straightforward.[26] For many years, members observed the fast in December instead of during the lunar month of Ramadan, based on founder Elijah Muhammad's pronouncements that fasting should be done at a time of the year when the days are short so as to make it easier and that doing so in December would help them move away from following Christian customs. Only in 1998 did the movement, now under the leadership of Louis Farrakhan, align its period of fasting with that of mainstream Islam.

Political Rituals

The term "political rituals," in Bell's terminology, denotes a "particularly loose genre" comprising activities that represent a particular group of people as the wielders of power and show their legitimacy. In the examples she provides (Bell 2009a: 128–9), such rituals both display and construct the power vested either in the central authorities of a society – kings and emperors, chiefs, governments – or in a particular subgroup. In a modern Western setting, political rituals are often

---

[25] See, e.g., https://krishna.com/wonderful-prasadam. In Sanskrit, prasāda can refer to any offering to a deity, including nonmaterial offerings of prayers. The offering of food can more specifically be referred to as naivedya, but prasada is also used as a term for the return gift of the deity, and ISKCON terminology follows this particular usage of the term. See Pinkney (2018).

[26] Ramadan: Fasting Strengthens Discipline, *The Final Call* (August 25, 2009), www.finalcall .com/artman/publish/Minister_Louis_Farrakhan_9/Fasting_strengthens_discipline_3939.shtml.

manifestations of civil religion, that is, practices and concepts that transcend those of particular religious communities and focus on the nation itself as an object of veneration. Examples of such practices include raising the national flag and singing the national anthem, holding military parades, swearing in a new head of state, and commemorating historical events that are considered to have defined the identity of the nation. NRMs are by their very nature not the religions of rulers or of the majority of a country's population, nor do they usually represent a powerful group within the host society. Political rituals staged by NRMs can nevertheless display their (real or perceived) powerful social position and reinforce their collective identity. The Million Man March, for example, was a mass rally held on October 16, 1995, at the initiative of Louis Farrakhan involving the gathering of several hundred thousand African American men on and around the National Mall in Washington, DC, one of the most iconic sites in the US capital. Although its purpose was to shine a spotlight on social and economic factors that impact the lives of Black people, a number of the main speakers represented a range of religious communities, including several Christian Churches. The highly symbolic nature of the venue and the fact that Farrakhan conceived of the idea for the event projected him and his organization into the limelight.

NRMs commonly live in a state of tension in relation to their host society, and some can use ritualized means to demonstrate their rejection of various aspects of mainstream culture. We find an example in the case of the Raëlian movement, which has held numerous demonstrations, ranging from anti-war rallies to protests against the Catholic Church – events characterized by a leading scholar as deliberate attempts to gain publicity by being controversial enough to attract the attention of the media (Palmer 2004: 67). An organization with far more strident opposition to mainstream norms is the Westboro Baptist Church, which, despite its name, is an organization independent of other Baptist denominations and characterized by a set of distinctive beliefs and practices instituted by its founder Fred Phelps (1929–2014).[27] Its doctrinal foundation is a Calvinist belief that humanity exists in a state of total depravity and that most people are predestined to eternal torment in hell. God's wrath, from the perspective of this movement, is in particular triggered by same-sex relations, and congregants take it upon themselves to proclaim to the world that God is punishing people for what they regard as the ultimate sin. Calamities ranging from earthquakes to epidemics are seen as resulting from God's anger, and the group chooses extremely provocative ways to disseminate this message to the public. Hence, their conviction that the deaths of US military personnel sent on missions abroad are caused by a God who punishes a country that has increasingly

---

[27] On this movement, see Barret-Fox (2016).

come to accept homosexuality has led them to picket the funerals of soldiers, carrying offensive banners with texts that celebrate military deaths as a sign of the power a wrathful deity has to inflict punishment.

Rituals rejecting the political order are particularly common in colonial and postcolonial contexts, and here we find organizations that combine political and religious aims as a means of resistance. The Mau Mau movement, which had its largest base among the Gikuyu-speaking people of the Kenyan highlands during the 1950s, can serve as an illustration. Two oath-taking rituals bound members together into a close-knit community whose secrets they swore not to disclose to outsiders. Initiates would participate in a sequence of ritualized activities that combined elements drawn from older Gikuyu rites of passage, such as passing through an archway made of banana plants and sugarcane, with the pronouncement of vows imbued with political aspirations, such as promising to obey the leaders of the movement and to avoid drinking beer and smoking cigarettes that had been manufactured by Europeans.[28]

In the most extreme cases, rejection of the social and political values of opponents has led to spectacular public displays of ritualized violence. Some of the most notorious examples in the twenty-first century have been those staged by militant Islamist and jihadist groups which, depending on how one defines the term, can be regarded as NRMs, as, for example, Reuven Firestone does (2012). To quote Firestone, the rather elastic term "jihadist" denotes "a transnational movement of militant Sunni Muslim activists, often called *jihadis*, who feel that they must be engaged in a prolonged and perhaps even endless war with the forces of evil defined vaguely as the West, or the 'Judeo-Christian' or 'Crusader-Zionist' enemy" (Firestone 2012: 264). The political goals of such groups are frequently vaguely formulated and are expressed through various means, such as mediatized displays of power and brutality. Here, we can turn to an organization known by various names, including ISIS, the Islamic State, and Daesh. While notorious for its genocidal policies regarding various ethnic and religious groups, what are arguably the most direct examples of ritualized violence are videos of executions produced as propaganda. A hallmark of ISIS was that acts generally condemned by the international community as war crimes, and which would therefore usually be hidden and denied by those committing them, were justified in religious terms and intentionally captured on film to be subsequently distributed by the organization itself.

Although we have in this section focused on the function of various rituals, this subsection on political rituals illustrates in particularly striking fashion that, like the myths we surveyed in Section 1, rituals can express the ideology of

---

[28] See Green (1990) for a detailed analysis.

a particular religious group. The fact that NRMs are minorities within their host societies entails that the rituals their members perform will be expressions of their allegiance to a different set of values than those of the majority. ISKCON members who worship Krishna by participating in a temple ritual are not only engaged in an act of devotion but are also displaying their rejection of the perceived materialism of mainstream society. A person afflicted with chronic pain who decides to consult a practitioner of Reiki healing is no doubt primarily concerned with finding relief from their affliction, but the choice to seek help from a version of complementary and alternative medicine rather than from the biomedical system can implicitly also be an ideological statement of rejecting mainstream medical care as deficient. New religions comprise the same range of rituals as their more traditional counterparts, but their heterodox status within their host societies makes the rituals of NRMs differ in significant ways from those of the dominant religions.

3 Material Objects in New Religious Movements

Religion, to quote the website of the journal *Material Religion*, "happens in material culture." Members of religious groups, depending upon the case in question, make images the focal point of devotional practices, congregate in buildings, dance, sing, treat their senses to foodstuffs prepared for religiously significant occasions, and adorn their bodies with various kinds of ornamentation. In other words, religion can be experienced through a wide variety of concrete ways. After having surveyed some genres of ritual activity in the preceding section, we now turn our attention to the role of objects as essential elements of the material cultures of new religions and will begin our journey of exploration with an illustrative example.

Tama-Re was the name given to a large collection of buildings in Georgia that belonged to the Nuwaubian Nation, an African American NRM originally called Ansar Pure Sufi. It was founded in 1967 by Dr. Malachi Z. York (b. 1945 as Dwight York), a musician and writer from New York. In 2005, Tama-Re was seized by local authorities, and the structures built by the Nuwaubians were eventually demolished. But while it was in operation as the headquarters of the movement, the massive Egyptian-themed complex was home to two pyramids, a sphinx, an obelisk, and statues of animal-headed deities, as well as to more incongruous elements like a crucified Black Jesus wearing a feather headdress in the style of the Native American peoples of the Great Plains.[29] The attire favored by Nuwabians at Tama-Re added to what might have seemed an exotic impression. Some wore Islamic-style clothing, while others sported outfits

---

[29] On the Nuwaubian movement, see Palmer (2010). The Tama-Re complex is described on pp. 71–4.

inspired by ideas about ancient Egypt. Pictures of York dating from the time the site was in operation show him wearing such distinctive accessories and garments as a black fez with a six-pointed star and ankh on it as well as a white robe reminiscent of those found in images depicting ancient Egyptian priests.

These architectural and sartorial choices reveal the influences of both the Nuwaubians' eclectic belief system as well as of the life of the movement's founder. As pointed out by scholar of religions Susan Palmer, through combining bits and pieces borrowed from, or inspired by, such diverse sources as Sufism, Black gnostic nationalism, trance messages received by Edgar Cayce, conspiracy theories, and UFO religions, the visual elements touched upon earlier highlight in particular the mythical history of African Americans as understood by York (Palmer 2010: 1). The Egyptian theme is tied to a version of the movement's origin myth that traces the roots of Black people through an ancient Nubian kingdom in Sudan and back to Egypt. York's fez stems from his days as a member of the Moorish Science Temple of America, whose founder, Noble Drew Ali (1886–1929), spread teachings about what he claimed was the true spiritual heritage of African Americans. Iconographic features reminiscent of Native American cultures, to take another example, are connected with both a phase in the movement's history during which they identified as "Yamassee Native American Moors" as well as York's claim of having been a descendant of Pocahontas (Palmer 2010: 7, 13).

The case of the Nuwaubian Nation illustrates a fundamental point about how religions function. The material objects that it created and with which it surrounded itself are, in a fundamental sense, precisely that: mere objects. A pyramid is but a three-dimensional geometric shape. A sacred statue is a sculpture more or less like any other similarly produced item. A religiously significant garment is just a piece of clothing. What differentiates objects considered to be special in some way within a particular religious community is the way in which they are framed. Narratives constructed around them and rituals in which they are set apart from mundane items create links to a postulated ultimate reality, which may or may not include such elements as gods, spirits, demons, karma, forces, destiny, and energies. This reality, at least to the uninitiated or untrained, is invisible and intangible. While some may claim to have had visions of various kinds or to have had other sorts of firsthand experiences of the normally imperceptible, material objects for many if not most members of NRMs constitute a key means by which the postulated ultimate reality, whatever it might consist of, acquires a tangible form. In other words, and to take an example, a depiction of a goddess or god, whether it is perceived by the beholder to be a representation or an actual manifestation, is the closest most members of a religious community will ever get to encountering that deity.

Prominent members of religious movements may indicate their close relationship to the divine or demonstrate their exceptional degree of piety and saintliness in concrete ways, by wearing emblems and articles of clothing. The nature of these objects shows how material items reveal immaterial qualities; they function as social labels that speak clearly of the place people have within a given social order. Those in positions of power often distinguish themselves from rank-and-file members by adopting a distinctive style of dress and by displaying insignia associated with their exalted status. The ornate costumes worn by Malachi Z. York clearly served this purpose by setting him apart as charismatic leader of the Nuwaubian movement.

Material objects can play a key role in constructing and representing the collective identity of a group. The Egyptian-themed symbolism and architecture of the Nuwaubian community and the distinctive dress style of its inhabitants served as such markers, and the effect could only have been all the more powerful given the location of Tama-Re in rural Georgia. Other functions fulfilled by material objects are practical in nature. Religious buildings can serve as settings for the performing of rituals and may also comprise living quarters offering a refuge from the rest of the world for the most dedicated members or the leadership of a movement. Mundane objects constructed for everyday activities may be designed in distinctive ways instantly recognizable to members as connected to the "brand" of their movement. Material objects can also secure some of the cash flow needed by an organization to carry out its daily operations, such as the gold pyramid at Tama-Re, which was home to a bookshop. The examples that follow will provide further illustrations of the often quite extensive array of objects produced within NRMs and the functions they fulfill.

Religious Buildings

As we have seen in connection with the case of the Tama-Re site, some of the most spectacular and costly material objects created by religious movements are buildings. Examples are numerous, and NRMs having access to generous funding or volunteer labor can produce quite massive structures. Here, we could name several examples among many: the ISKCON Temple of the Vedic Planetarium that at the time of writing is being constructed in the Indian city of Mayapur; the Osho International Meditation Resort located in the Indian city of Pune; and Scientology's Flag Service Organization in Clearwater, Florida. Each of these organizational homes is built, or at least imagined, on the grandest of scales.

As the following will show, the distinctive architecture and décor of buildings like these often function as the visible expressions of a movement's ideology. At the same time, these structures can also serve various practical functions in their roles as venues for ritual activities, spaces for members to gather, and homes for seemingly secular entities such as shops and administrative headquarters.

Founded in 1976 by Oberto Airaudi (1950–2013), the spiritual community of Damanhur located in the foothills of the Italian Alps is a striking example of a concrete, and grandiose, expression of the founder's cosmological views, which have been described as "New Age" (Pace 2000: 575; Zoccatelli 2016: 147). Here, one finds large subterranean spaces given names like the Hall of Spheres, the Hall of Mirrors, and the Hall of the Earth, all of which were excavated by hand and are decorated with murals, mosaics, and other works of art. Other structures are far simpler, for instance the so-called Stone Circuits, where colored stones meander across the grass in paths that correspond to the energy lines that are said to be part of the landscape. The striking visual culture of the community has an obvious aesthetic effect and embodies Airaudi's ideas about the cosmos and everything in it. Meanwhile, since Damanhur attracts numerous visitors, the constructions also help generate some of the funds needed to help keep the movement alive. Various types of tours are organized by the community, and these are later reviewed just as any other tourist attraction would be on sites like Tripadvisor.

The headquarters of a somewhat older new religion, Anthroposophy, similarly combines ideological and practical functions. This movement was founded in the last days of 1912 by the Austrian esotericist Rudolf Steiner after he broke his longstanding ties with the Theosophical Society.[30] In addition to presenting the details of an elaborate cosmology in which numerous spiritual beings influence or direct events in world history, Steiner also helped launch or shape many practical applications that build on his ideas, one of which is an instantly recognizable architectural style. The international headquarters of the movement is a large building known as the Goetheanum, located near the Swiss city of Basel.[31] One way of understanding Anthroposophy is to view it as a kind of counterculture that arose in response to a perceived threat from a mainstream society that was seen as becoming increasingly materialistic. The distinctive shape of its central building, the Goetheanum – the construction of which began in 1925 – reflects this oppositional stance. Contrary to the modernist and

---

[30] For a thorough survey of Steiner's involvement with the Theosophical Society, his work during this period, and his break with the organization, see Zander (2007: 545–780).

[31] The Goetheanum was conceived as a successor to the Johannesbau, a building on the same site that was built in 1913 and renamed Goetheanum in 1917, that burned down on New Year's Eve in 1922. The present-day building is therefore also referred to as the second Goetheanum. On Steiner's views on art and architecture, see Ohlenschläger (1999), Zander (2007: 1063–1180); and Zander (2019: 134–6).

functionalist architecture that emerged as an important trend in the early twentieth century, a style that emphasized straight lines and eschewed ornamentation, the Goetheanum building is characterized by curved shapes reminiscent of expressionistic art. The shapes and colors were intended to generate a feeling of being connected to the spiritual world in those who visited the structure (Zander 2007: 1119). This particular architectural style has since become an identity marker of the Anthroposophical movement, and countless other buildings with characteristically curved rather than straight lines have been constructed in order to house Waldorf schools and other institutions building upon Steiner's legacy. The Goetheanum is a manifestation of the Anthroposophical movement in other ways as well. It is the home of the School of Spiritual Science, a body that insiders to the movement define as "an institution intended to be an esoteric school for spiritual scientific research and study"[32] but which an outside observer might characterize as a central locus of doctrinal production.[33] Another purpose it serves is as a venue for performances of works of central importance within the Anthroposophical community, such as Goethe's *Faust* and Steiner's mystery dramas. The latter consist of a set of four highly stylized stage productions that follow a group of karmically connected individuals over the course of several incarnations. In addition to the aforementioned, the gargantuan structure serves as an apt illustration of the double function of many religious buildings, alluded to in the beginning of this subsection, since it also contains a bookstore, a library, exhibition halls, office spaces, conference rooms, and a cafe.

Iconography

Religious iconography comes in many forms: from paintings, drawings, and sculptures to – in more recent times – photographs, films, and video sequences. It can represent otherwise rather abstract cosmological concepts, and it can present stylized depictions of a movement's key figures or its postulated suprahuman entities. It can also illustrate or present stories in non-scriptural formats. The iconography of new traditions, just like that of more traditional ones, can be understood in a variety of ways. It may be perceived as actual

---

[32] Quoted from www.rudolfsteiner.org/school#:~:text=%20School%20for%20Spiritual% 20Science%20%201%20General,science%20%E2%80%93%20biology%2C%20physics%2C %20chemistry%20%E2%80%93... %20More%20 (accessed on 20 November 2020).

[33] Given Steiner's insistence that the activities of this organization constitute a form of science, one could also view the various sections in which it is divided as being departments, the School of Spiritual Science as a kind of university, and the Goetheanum itself as a campus. This, too, it should be stressed, is an outsider's view, since Anthroposophists can explicitly reject this characterization; see Schmidt (2010: 99).

manifestations of the divine, representations of spiritual realities, objects of worship, or art. A few examples follow.

Abstract cosmologies can be made more concrete by being represented visually. One of many post-Theosophical religious entrepreneurs, Martinus (1890–1981, born Martinus Thomsen but normally referred to by his first name only), was a Danish prophet who combined occultist and Theosophical ideas with Christian motifs. He produced a set of one hundred iconographic representations of his cosmological concepts. These images combine the didactic (in that they can be used to explain his cosmology) and the aesthetic (as they are constructed of brightly colored geometric shapes and can be appreciated for their visual impression) while simultaneously serving as identity markers (since visitors to the homes of people who study his teachings may find the walls adorned with poster-sized reproductions of these motifs; these are sold in the movement's administrative headquarters in Copenhagen). Their function as tools to help make a dense set of complex concepts more comprehensible is made clear by the fact that every color and shape has a specific meaning which accompanying texts spell out in detail. We can take as an example an image called the Principle of World Redemption, also known as Symbol No. 2.[34] A fundamental belief within the movement is that religions can be conceptualized as rungs on an evolutionary ladder and that humanity will one day reach a stage of spiritual advancement where religions will be superseded by the logical and scientific insights Martinus offered. The Principle of World Redemption illustrates this idea of spiritual progress through its stylized depiction of a staircase over which a star emanating three rays hovers. At the bottom of the staircase, the rays are orange, symbolizing "lower" religions; toward the middle, they are yellow, representing religions deemed higher, such as Christianity, Islam, and Buddhism; and at the top of the staircase, they are white, the color of "cosmic science, which will replace all the world's religions. Cosmic science is absolute truth."

Likenesses of key figures are ubiquitous in the spaces new religious movements create and maintain. Portraits of Rudolf Steiner adorn walls in Anthroposophical institutions the world over. Pictures of L. Ron Hubbard can be found on display in every local branch of the Church of Scientology. Founder A. C. Bhaktivedanta Swami Prabhupada is omnipresent throughout the ISKCON milieu in a number of forms. Potential readers meet his gaze on the back covers of numerous books. Prabhupada-shaped statues dwell in temples and prominently displayed photographs can be

---

[34] The symbol described here and the quote at the end of the paragraph can be found at www
.martinus.dk/en/martinus-symbols/symbol-overview/symbol-2/index.html.

found in the homes of ISKCON members. Another form in which he is present in such settings is through true-to-life-size castings of his feet. The role of the guru's "lotus feet," as they are referred to by ISKCON devotees, is linked to the centrality of that particular figure in the movement. As Prabhupada explained in his commentary on a passage of the Srimad Bhagavatam (4.26.20), "Touching the lotus feet of a spiritual master means giving up one's false prestige and unnecessarily puffed-up position in the material world."

An important function of iconography is to render visible what generally escapes detection by the human eye, such as inhabitants of culturally postulated suprahuman realms. Different movements will, of course, have very different ways of envisioning these entities, which may or may not include the gods, angels, and demons often associated with older religions. One particular conception that fits squarely in a modern context such as ours presumes the existence of extraterrestrial beings. Iconography characteristic not only of religious movements based on such beliefs but also of the broader cultic milieu where space aliens figure prominently typically features depictions not only of these beings but also of the vehicles they use as modes of transportation. Ideas about so-called flying saucers spread via the media following a widely publicized sighting on June 24, 1947, of what was purported to be a UFO.[35] Kenneth Arnold (1915–1984), an amateur pilot, claimed that he had spotted nine shiny objects passing Mount Rainier at high speed when he was flying his small plane. Once the story was picked up, Arnold became an instant celebrity. Soon afterward, additional voices were heard as others came forward to share their stories of having had contact with space aliens who arrived in such vessels. One of the earliest of these contactees was George Adamski (1891–1965), who would become well known for his photos of UFOs. With the emergence of contactee culture, UFO lore took a religious turn, which makes Adamski, who had an interest in the occult, a relevant figure to consider. In 1934, he became the leader of the Royal Order of Tibet, a small group of individuals having connections to Theosophy but, after Arnold's sighting, Adamski's focus shifted to interplanetary visits, and in the years that followed, Adamski reported having spotted a large number of unidentified flying objects. He also claimed to have met a Venusian named Orthon, who had come to Earth to relay a message to humanity via Adamski warning of the dire consequences that would result from continued nuclear armament. Adamski shared a picture he said he had taken of the shuttle ship that had transported Orthon; the slightly grainy photograph, which shows what appears to be the top half of a sphere with three round landing

---

[35] On the history of UFO beliefs, see Denzler (2003).

struts sticking out of it, has since become one of the most widely reproduced UFO images. Critics, however, later identified the apparent landing gear as nothing more exotic than three ordinary General Electric lightbulbs, and various guesses have been made regarding what precisely comprised the main component of Adamski's purported UFO. Perhaps, it has been suggested, it was part of a chicken brooder, a streetlight, or the reflector-shade of a gas lantern.

Not only are depictions of UFOs now commonplace but images of the beings operating them have also become instantly recognizable staples of popular culture, in particular those called greys, which are usually presented as rather small, humanoid creatures with hairless bodies, greyish skin, and large, black eyes. This particular way of envisioning visitors from outer space became widespread after Betty and Barney Hill came forward with a story about a series of events that they claimed had transpired in connection with having spotted a UFO in September of 1961 while driving home from a vacation. After the sighting, the couple were plagued by anxiety and eventually sought professional help. During a series of hypnosis sessions, a far more detailed story of their encounter emerged involving having been abducted and taken aboard a spaceship by a group of large-eyed humanoid creatures and thereafter subjected to a series of humiliating and unpleasant examinations. Their tale reached a very large audience, first through newspaper articles focusing on the Hills' claims and then later in 1966 when author John G. Fuller published an account in his book *The Interrupted Journey*. The greyish humanoids have since become prototypical images of what visitors from another planet might look like and they have been represented innumerable times in drawings (including a sketch on the cover of *The Interrupted Journey*) and on film, including documentaries purporting to contain footage of actual aliens.

While it is common knowledge that videos and photographs can be manipulated, they seem nevertheless to have an air of facticity about them that religious insiders can find compelling – yet at the same time opens the door for debunking by critics. The situation is quite different, however, when it comes to the many forms of iconography where no claims are made about the products being exact representations of a suprahuman dimension. Art in particular has been a favored medium for some religious groups. For example, Oberto Airaudi produced paintings before he founded Damanhur, and art has retained its prominent position within the community. Other leaders of NRMs and ordinary members alike have created iconographic works that, it may be argued, can also be classified as art.[36] The role these and similar creative endeavors play in the material culture of a movement seems in part to be connected to historically

---

[36] For a background discussion, see Introvigne (2016).

contingent factors, such as the personal interests of the founders and prominent members, and in part to the attraction that the religious ideology holds for artists who may otherwise be unaffiliated with it. Hence, some families of religions – and here, to take but one example, movements connected in some way to Theosophy have a particularly strong track record – seem to foster an interest in art more than others.

Anthroposophy, perhaps the most important post-Theosophical movement, has inspired countless artists since founder Rudolf Steiner launched his career as a spiritual teacher in the first quarter of the twentieth century. The abstract art of Swedish painter Hilma af Klint (1862–1944) is closely linked to her involvement with such turn-of-the-century organizations as the Anthroposophical Society and has in the twenty-first century received much attention. The sheer volume of work produced by other people with links to the Anthroposophical movement – ranging from paintings, drawings, woodcuts, textiles, and sculptures to furniture, clocks, and jewelry – is so staggering that a massive volume published in 2015 by Reinhold J. Fäth and David Voda could present 125 such artists. Even the use of a particular font on packing materials makes Anthroposophical products instantly recognizable. If one were so inclined, it would doubtlessly be possible to adorn or fill every aspect of one's life, including each of its pivotal moments, with objects that form part of Anthroposophical material culture. Since these objects are shaped in accordance with aesthetic principles that can be traced back to what are understood to be Steiner's clairvoyantly perceived insights, they serve as iconographic representations of the movement's ideas and, in more this-wordly terms, as its brand.

Clothing

Some movements prescribe, or may even require, adopting a particular style of dress during the performance of rituals or throughout the day in general. This ideal may include having a particular hairstyle or acquiring a specific set of accessories. Male members of ISKCON, for example, in addition to applying *tilak* markings to their bodies may also wear white or saffron-colored Indian-style clothing. The specifics of their choices will be based upon such factors as level of engagement within the organization and if the attire is to be worn during a ritual. Many members wear strands of small wooden beads from the tulsi tree around their neck. Some sport a special hairstyle with a tuft preserved on the back of an otherwise completely shaved or closely cropped head. They may have a small cloth bag containing a set of prayer beads (a *mala*) with them. This accessory is for many devotees an indispensable tool because it aids them in carrying out the central element of ISKCON ritual practice throughout the day, namely chanting the Hare Krishna mantra.

The manner of dress favored within the ISKCON movement clearly recalls the aesthetics and symbolism of its Indian, Vaishnava roots. NRMs having a more tenuous historical relationship to earlier traditions may adopt a particular style created by their founders that reflects their own at times quite idiosyncratic ideas. Here, the Osho movement can serve as an example. It was started by Chandra Mohan Jain (1931–1990, later known by several other names, including Bhagwan Shree Rajneesh and Osho), a Jain from central India. For many years, it was known as the Rajneesh movement because of a nickname given to its founder. Despite his cultural roots, its practices constitute a panoply of meditation techniques and experiential group activities that are very eclectic and are in particular inspired by the human potential movement. Rajneesh/Osho instituted a style of clothing that was worn by members during much of the 1970s and 1980s and appears to have been his own invention (Chryssides 1999: 208). It was so striking that his followers were at the time nicknamed "orange people" because of the hues of their garments. Another defining element of their particular mode of dressing was wearing a necklace with a photograph of Rajneesh attached to it.

In the cases of ISKCON and the Rajneesh movement, clothing styles were adopted which deviated radically from those prevalent within mainstream Western societies. In contrast, other movements have imbued what are generally common forms of dress in their host cultures with new meanings. One example is the maritime outfit worn by members of Scientology's top clergy, the so-called Sea Org. Founded in 1967, this organization within an organization received its name because its members were stationed on three ships then serving as the movement's headquarters. Although much of the Sea Org's operations are now land-based, the tradition of wearing naval-style uniforms, which distinguish wearers according to a ranking system that borrows liberally from military terminology, remains.[37]

An institutionalized adoption of the dress code of a segment of majority society can be seen in the case of missionaries deployed by the Church of Jesus Christ of Latter-day Saints. Their attire is strictly regulated and conforms to what would in an American context be seen as conservative values.[38] Depending upon where they are stationed, male missionaries are expected to wear either a suit or at the very least a white shirt and a tie. Any exceptions to the rule will be instituted in top-down fashion by the mission president. Such a centralized way of managing

---

[37] On the history and role of the Sea Org, see Urban (2011: 122–5).

[38] See, e.g., www.churchofjesuschrist.org/callings/missionary/guidelines-for-elders?lang=eng.in

sartorial matters results in missionaries not adapting to local customs when abroad other than in regard to practical issues like wearing heavy jackets in cold climates or hats in places where protection from the sun is of vital importance. While wearing a suit and tie in much of the United States signals conservative values and allows one to blend in, in countries with far more casual dress codes like Denmark and Sweden, following such guidelines causes one to stand out in a way that arguably may not have the desired effect.

Redescribing the Natural World

Thus far, we have discussed examples of material objects created by NRMs to serve functions ranging from the ideological to the practical. Presumably, any kind of object can be transformed by the religious imagination and, once imbued with new significance, ultimately become an integral part of a group's material culture. This includes, of course, naturally occurring objects and structures. Stones said to have various spiritual or healing properties are common staples found on display in many New Age shops, health food stores, and wellness fairs. A customer may be advised to buy amethyst if they wish to fend off negative energy or are in need of healing. Rose quartz might be recommended if there is a broken heart to be mended. However, as is hardly surprising in a spiritual milieu with no single locus of authority, the properties attributed to various crystals, as they are often called, differ from book to book, group to group, and website to website.

Entire features of a landscape, once redescribed, can become centerpieces of religious imagination. For instance, the town of Visoko, located in Bosnia and Herzegovina, has in recent years become a New Age site due to claims made by the Bosnian-American entrepreneur Semir Osmanagić suggesting that it is home to mysterious structures built thousands of years ago by an advanced civilization (Hammer & Swartz 2020). Over time, his claims have transformed several naturally occurring geological features into ancient pyramids and tunnels constructed by means of a technology that enabled those early engineers to direct potent healing energies – at least in the minds of visitors, helpers, and watchers of YouTube videos from all over the world. Onsite guides provide a bare-bones narrative explaining the nature and history of the place and the alleged beneficial effects of spending time there. Within this framework, passageways an outside observer might interpret as mine shafts or as the result of various excavation projects carried out at the complex become tunnels dug out some 30,000 years ago by an unknown civilization. Stone blocks not differing in any obvious way from other rocks found there are presented as objects created to concentrate vital energies from the earth by means of quartz crystals embedded in them. Here, we find religiously tinged ideas about the properties of stones that, based on what, for outsiders might seem an opaque set of criteria, are seen as having exceptional qualities combined with another culturally widespread belief encountered within New Age milieus, namely that pyramids have special properties.

Redescribing Existing Artifacts

Just as naturally occurring objects like stones and hills can be imbued with religious significance and receive entirely new identities, existing artifacts can also be reimagined and redescribed. The examples that follow show how an ancient megalithic site can be interpreted as a monument associated with druids, and how fake Mesoamerican antiquities can be ascribed various paranormal powers and associated with aliens from outer space.

Stonehenge, a monument archaeologists understand as having been built and rebuilt in several phases beginning roughly in 3000 BCE, was first associated with the druids by antiquarians such as John Aubrey (1626–1697) in the seventeenth century.[39] The Ancient Order of Druids, a fraternal order having a special interest in druids and Celtic religion, became the first organization in modern times to conduct rituals at the site, which they did in 1905. A surge in the popularity of this practice accompanied the rise of the counterculture in the 1960s, and for several years Pagans gathered at Stonehenge in the days around the summer solstice. The British authorities clamped down on the religious use of Stonehenge in 1985, as the site is owned by the Crown, but restrictions have been eased to some extent since then. However, regardless of whether Pagans are permitted to celebrate their rituals there, Stonehenge occupies a sacralized place within the religious imagination that has little in common with what is known by archaeologists about its roots in prehistory.

A religiously motivated reinterpretation of a very different kind has given a set of particularly striking objects – this time likenesses of human skulls made from large chunks of translucent quartz – an imaginary history that appeals to some individuals within New Age milieus.[40] Whereas Stonehenge is a 5,000-year-old monument that is redescribed as being several millennia younger, the crystal skulls are modern artifacts whose origins are conceptually projected far back in time and are thus made much older. It has been estimated that these crystal skulls first started being produced in the mid-nineteenth century, a time when there was a brisk trade in fake Mexican antiques. Laboratory analyses of these objects have shown that they were made using modern power tools, and no credible evidence exists to suggest that they actually are of Mesoamerican

---

[39] Modern reinterpretations of Stonehenge are surveyed in Hutton (2009).

[40] The story of the crystal skulls is briefly surveyed in Walsh (2008). MacLaren Walsh & Topping (2018) is a detailed biography of the French arts dealer Eugène Boban, who sold the first of these fakes.

origin. Despite these assessments, specialized New Age literature, which sometimes refers to them by proper names, treats them as ancient objects that are in some way conscious and capable of acting with intent. They are attributed with various supernatural abilities, such as being able to communicate via telepathy, and occasionally receive ritualized treatment similar to what one would see in the case of sacred objects in more traditional religions.

Such examples as the interest in pyramid-shaped hills, colored stones, and crystal skulls one finds in sectors of the cultic milieu illustrate how fundamental objects can be in the emergence of new religious phenomena. A stone or a fake Mesoamerican artifact does not, as some more conventional views of religion might have it, "express" a religious belief (cf. Morgan 2010: 1–7). Rather, striking objects can be the focal point around which a variety of quite diverse and malleable opinions and ritualized behaviors can coalesce.

4 Texts

New religious movements tend to yield a vast textual output. Some, for instance, publish biographies of their founders, and one of the most voluminous examples of this genre is ISKCON's presentation of the life of its founder, *Srila Prabhupada Lilamrta*, a story that takes seven volumes to tell (Goswami 1980). Occasionally, leaders will write their own autobiographies, such as the regrettably incomplete ones penned by Rudolf Steiner and Alice Bailey. In addition to these types of texts, there are histories produced by adherents of new religions, which consist of ideologically appropriate accounts of the development of their movements. The LDS Church has produced so much material of this sort that an entire website has been devoted to providing interested parties with reading suggestions as well as a searchable catalog of relevant materials.[41] Periodicals can also be mentioned in this context. Members of nineteenth-century Spiritualist and Theosophical milieus were pioneers in using them to disseminate their messages, as evidenced by the hundreds of titles listed on a digitized archive.[42] In the contemporary period, countless new religions produce such materials. Other forms of written output include inspirational messages to members, information put together for outsiders and especially for potential recruits, apologetic works defending the truth of the movement's doctrines, instructions for carrying out rituals, and much else besides. In the twenty-first century, more traditional forms of communication are supplemented by new media like websites, blogs, Facebook groups, audio files with lectures, and YouTube videos.

---

[41] https://history.churchofjesuschrist.org/?lang=eng.

[42] The archive in question is that of the International Association for the Preservation of Spiritualist and Occult Periodicals, available at iapsop.com.

Texts produced by NRMs will, like those of their older counterparts, typically belong to two or more tiers. The top tier will consist of a selection of writings from a larger corpus, ones considered by leading members of a particular movement to be the most sacred or most authoritative source of religious insight: in other words, its canonical works.[43] Such texts are at the confluence of all the themes that we have broached so far in this Element, and in them one will find, just as is the case with those of more traditional religions, presentations of new religious movements' myths, doctrines, and practices. The use of canonical works is often ritualized: they can be read during communal gatherings, or they can be recited as part of a liturgy. They are also material objects and as such can be venerated, printed in extravagantly produced editions or in more modest formats, handed out as gifts, or exchanged for money.

In many cases, texts that are of central importance for NRMs bear strong resemblance to those of much older religions. For example, numerous more or less recently established organizations see the Bible as the work most central to their tradition, while others may pick a selection of the innumerable writings of classical India as their points of reference. While new religions generally strike a balance between the recognizable ("we are a Christian group that regards the Bible as infallible") and the innovative ("contrary to other groups, we have understood the true message of the Bible"), some will present entirely new texts brought into being through prophetic means.

This section will first take up cases of how pre-existing textual canons have been reinterpreted. We will continue by providing examples of new scriptures. Some of the instances we include in this section are of a perhaps unexpected phenomenon: religions that refer to texts that, according to the usual standards of empirical evidence, exist solely as products of the human imagination. While these texts are referred to by title, and while their contents have been summarized and quoted in other texts, the actual volumes themselves have presumably never existed in physical form. Lastly, we conclude by returning to the topic of how religious texts can figure in rituals and function as material objects.

Reinterpreting Older Texts

Once a canon has been fixed, challenges will inevitably arise, which is in part due to the fact that texts need to be interpreted anew as time passes if they are to retain their relevance. Many NRMs give existing texts the status of canonical scripture but reuse them in creative ways by producing novel translations and instituting innovative commentarial traditions. In such cases, a religious elite

---

[43] On the concept of canons, see Smith (1982). On canonical texts in new religions, see Hammer & Rothstein (2012) and Gallagher (2014).

will have the double role of being both those who promote the movement's novel reading of the text as well as those who set boundaries against anyone who might wish to introduce further innovations. By implementing various measures, this elite can try to claim sole rights for reproducing the text, commenting upon it, and stipulating precisely which interpretations are to be considered legitimate. In a centralized movement, an organizational body consisting of leaders can impose such strictures. In less formally structured milieus, however, the interpretive elite may consist of entrepreneurial individuals who publish bestselling books.

For NRMs belonging to the Christian family of traditions, the Bible plays a crucial role in this process of controlled innovation. An example of a new translation that nudges the reader toward a particular understanding of the text that aligns with the doctrines of the movement is the so-called New World Translation of the Bible produced by the Jehovah's Witnesses. As can be deduced from the name of the organization, the deity's proper name, according to the group's foundational beliefs, is Jehovah. The movement thus adopts a reading of JHWH, the vowelless designation that appears thousands of times in the Hebrew Bible, that it and its New World Translation shares with a few other Bible translations. Similarly, the Witnesses rely in their translation of a key concept of the Christian tradition on the basic and most common meaning of the Greek word *staurós*, which is stake, rather than cross.[44] They eschew the word cross because they see it as the introduction of a pagan symbol into Christianity.[45]

There are limits, however, as to just how freely a translation can treat the original text lest it be roundly criticized by outsiders. It is therefore far easier to produce commentaries on passages that promote radically innovative understandings that can in some cases be light-years away from what earlier generations of Christians had in mind. Several movements belonging to the Theosophical family of religions embrace the notion that attaining a high level of spiritual insight or clairvoyant perception will allow one to decode "the true meaning" of biblical passages. They also insist that such understandings can differ dramatically from more literal readings. We find an example of this approach in a book entitled *Esoteric Christianity: The Lesser Mysteries*, which was written shortly after the turn of the twentieth century by Annie Besant (1847–1943) – Helena Blavatsky's successor as Theosophical leader.

---

[44] The perhaps best-known Greek dictionary, the Lidell, Scott, Jones *Ancient Greek Lexicon*, available at lsj.gr, lists "upright pale or stake" as the primary meaning of the word.

[45] For an assessment of the New World Translation, see Penton (2015: 249–53). The claim that the cross is a pagan symbol is found in sources such as www.jw.org/en/library/books/bible-teach/origin-cross-symbol-pagan/.

Esoteric Christianity discusses what Besant claimed to be the true nature of Christianity.[46] Readers of the volume, Besant asserts, aided by reason and the weight of historical evidence in favor of her case, will become convinced that the essence of Christianity is in actuality very different from the versions presented by the existing churches. Describing the exoteric form of the religion – that is, the one familiar to the masses – as an insult to the intelligence of modern people (Besant 1905: 38), she positions herself as one who can reveal and revive the higher truths, which are already there hiding in plain sight. These are the insights that can be found via a careful reading of the New Testament and the texts of the early church theologians.

Besant's claims are complex and therefore only a few elements can be touched upon here. One that is particularly striking is the distinction she makes between Jesus and Christ, two beings that are, according to her interpretation, separate. In her retelling, the former, in connection with his baptism in the river Jordan at the age of twenty-nine, became the vessel of the latter, a "glorious Being belonging to the great spiritual hierarchy that guides the spiritual evolution of humanity" (Besant, 1905: 140). Although this supernatural spark is what ignites his ministry, the various healing miracles attributed to him are, according to Besant, due to "magnetic energies" (1905: 135). In other words, instead of being produced by any exceptional means, they were in fact the result of powers possessed by all initiates of a certain level (1905: 145–6). After Jesus' physical death, his subtle spiritual body continued to visit his disciples for a period of fifty years, and it was during this time in particular, her narrative continues, that the mysteries of Christianity were revealed to them (1905: 137). A long and complicated set of arguments presented in chapter 5 of Besant's book leads her to the conclusion that the accounts given in the New Testament are veiled references to a series of actual events that transpired following the descent of a spiritual being, the Solar Logos, into matter. She also reveals an additional layer to the story – its role as a symbolic rendition of a process whereby Christ as a principle may be awakened in individuals who have advanced sufficiently in their spiritual development.

Perhaps less radical than attempts to infuse well-known works with new meanings are interpretations that link them to the present instead of their actual time of origin. Millennialist movements tend to be particularly prone to retroject-ing the present into the past. In this context, texts like the Book of Daniel or the Book of Revelation are not understood as being informed by the lives and times of those who wrote them but are rather interpreted in the light of the events of our own day and age. Furthermore, the Bible itself is viewed as a single, coherent

---

[46] For an analysis of the way in which Besant draws out a new meaning from select biblical passages, see Hammer (2019).

volume, rather than a collection of writings composed by a number of people from different time periods. Examples of such attempts to eke out the details of impending apocalyptic scenarios from biblical texts are numerous. The Jehovah's Witnesses, for instance, have in the past used clues from such textual passages to predict the date for when history would come to an end, and have over the years of the movement's existence announced that this would happen in 1914, 1925, and 1975 (Penton 2015: 277–81). Projections of Endtime scenarios are also commonly found in what could be characterized as a large, conservative Christian cultic milieu. Such depictions are typically based on the notion that God has an intricate plan for precisely how and when the world as we know it will come to an end. According to this perspective, a careful reading of various key passages in the Bible will yield information about a string of future events including the Rapture (i.e., the belief, stemming from 1 Thessalonians 4:17, that the faithful will disappear from the Earth and miraculously be taken up in the heavens); the rule of a sinister figure referred to as Antichrist (mentioned in the First Epistle and Second Epistle of John); and Armageddon, a cataclysmic battle between the forces of good and evil that will take place at a site in the present nation of Israel (referred to in Revelation 16:16).

The innovative potential of new translations and commentaries is, of course, present in non-Christian religions as well. Here, the Bhagavad Gita can serve as an example from the Hindu family of traditions. Founders of various movements, such as Swami Prabhupada (ISKCON), Paramahamsa Yogananda (the Self-Realization Fellowship), and Maharishi Mahesh Yogi (Transcendental Meditation), have produced English-language versions of the text, either in its entirety or selections from it, that reflect their respective doctrines. If we consider the ISKCON version, for instance, we find that its seemingly neutral title, *Bhagavad-Gītā As It Is*, obfuscates the fact that its contents are the product of a particular interpretative tradition rooted in Bengali Vaishnavism.[47]

Creating New Scriptures

While some NRMs and religious milieus, as we have seen, reinterpret existing canonical texts in creative ways, others present entirely new ones. Since these writings generally lack the air of authority that tends to surround more traditional canonical works, they are often buttressed by a secondary textual layer that attempts to explain the importance of the work and legitimize its content. This fortifying layer may include separately published apologetic works, justifying additions such as a preface or footnotes, and self-referential passages extolling the text's virtues.

---

[47] On modern Gita translations more generally, see Davis (2015: 154–77).

New authoritative texts are commonly, within their respective traditions, understood as resulting from communication with a suprahuman source. Examples abound in the recorded history of religions, and in recent decades they are often referred to as channeled texts (Brown 1997). To name but a few, we could mention (in roughly chronological order) *Oahspe: A New Bible* (1882), *The Urantia Book* (published in 1955 but mediumistically "received" in the second half of the 1920s or the first half of the 1930s), *Seth Speaks* (1972), and *Conversations with God, Book 1: An Uncommon Dialogue* (1995).

One of the most widely distributed of these works – and one which does not belong to any specific NRM but instead is distributed throughout much of the New Age milieu – is the massive *A Course in Miracles*, often abbreviated as ACIM.[48] This three-volume work was "scribed" over the course of several years by psychologist Helen Schucman (1909–1981), typed out and edited for publication by her and her colleague William Thetford (1923–1988), and published in 1975. The sender of the text is simply identified as the Voice, but the implicit author is Jesus, and its language is infused with Christian terms such as Christ and Holy Spirit. This merely indicates the family of religions within which the message of ACIM can be positioned, however, since its contents would no doubt strike many Christian readers as quite unfamiliar. A perhaps somewhat bold and ambitious attempt to summarize with a few short sentences the basic message of a work consisting of more than 1,300 pages might run as follows: The world we experience with our everyday senses is in actuality a product of our own making and stems from being caught up in the painful illusion that we are somehow separated from the divine reality when in fact that is all there truly is. What ACIM can offer is a practical routine based on radical forgiveness intended to aid one in dismantling the erroneous perspective on the nature of reality that we have succumbed to. The multi-faceted secondary textual layer that surrounds this text consists of features such as a preface portraying Schucman as a rather reticent recipient of a message that did not accord with her way of life, and which therefore must have come from a transcendent source; it also includes self-referential statements emphasizing the unique importance of the book not just as "a course in miracles" but as "a required course." The foundation that holds the copyright attributes to the book an exceptional significance, calling it a "universal spiritual teaching."[49]

Another way of producing and promoting new texts involves claiming that they are in fact ancient but only first discovered now, a well-known phenomenon from other religions. Several Tibetan religious traditions, for instance,

---

[48] Taves (2016: 151–221) provides a study of the emergence of ACIM as a revelatory text.
[49] https://acim.org/about-acim/.

share the idea that various objects of great religious significance, including texts, were hidden away by spiritual masters of bygone ages and have been rediscovered by revelatory means in more recent historical times. The perhaps most obvious parallel in terms of NRMs is the case of the Book of Mormon, published in 1830 and purportedly translated from an ancient record telling of the fortunes of various peoples of Near Eastern origin said to have populated the Americas in the distant past. The virtual text here is the putative original, described as having been inscribed in Reformed Egyptian on a set of golden-colored metal sheets. The legitimizing secondary text is in this case the elaborate story that has taken shape concerning its discovery. According to this account, in 1823 the prophet Joseph Smith Jr. (1805–1844) was directed by an angel to a hill where a stone chest containing the plates had been buried. Although he visited the hill every year, he was only first permitted to retrieve them in 1827. Once the gold plates were in his possession, the story goes, he at first did not allow anybody else to see them. Only later were testimonies gathered from a select group of people who had been permitted to handle and view them. An English-language counterpart was eventually produced by means of supernatural processes involving instruments such as a so-called seer stone and what could be characterized as prophetic eyeglasses that he called the Urim and Thummim.

The story of James Strang and the Voree plates illustrates the way in which the purported discovery of an ancient text by suprahuman means is perceived as plausible only within the confines of a particular movement.[50] After the death of Joseph Smith, the young church was in a crisis regarding the matter of succession. While most members followed Brigham Young (1801–1877), some decided to place their loyalties with other leaders. One of the smaller of these splinter groups accepted James J. Strang (1813–1856) as Smith's true spiritual heir. He supported his claim to being the new prophet, seer, and revelator of the Mormons by referring to a story quite like the one told by Joseph Smith. Strang related that an angel of God had revealed to him that records prepared by an ancient Native American, Rajah Manchou of Vorito, were buried in a hillside near Voree, Wisconsin. After having dug a few feet into the ground, Strang and his companions discovered three small brass plates engraved on both sides. Four of the surfaces were covered with what appeared to be a mysterious script. The remaining two consisted of a map and some images. Acting in his capacity as prophet, Strang translated the text portion in 1845. Contrary to Smith's treatment of the golden plates he reported finding, Strang made the items he

---

[50] An account of the events summarized here and facsimile reproductions of the Voree plates can be found at https://archive.ph/20120917103244/http://www.strangite.org/Plates.htm.

found available for inspection. In 1851 he presented a new translation, this time in the form of an extensive text titled Book of the Law of the Lord, purportedly a rendition of the so-called Plates of Laban that had been in the possession of Nephi, a major character in the Book of Mormon. Seven witnesses furthermore testified that they had seen the original Plates of Laban. Whereas the existence of the gold plates and the accuracy of Joseph Smith's rendition of these have become accepted doctrines of the LDS Church, a church with seventeen million members at the time of writing, Strang's story is rejected by the majority Mormon institution and is part of the founding mythology of the small Strangite splinter group, a community of some 300 members.

Although the Mormon family of denominations may be the most widely known tradition where a purportedly ancient text unknown to outsiders serves as its foundational document, there are other examples. In 1888, the creator of the Theosophical worldview, Helena Blavatsky (1831–1891), presented a complex cosmology and a rambling narrative about the place of humans in that cosmos in a massive two-volume work, *The Secret Doctrine*. Blavatsky did not position herself as the originator of these teachings but rather as a transmitter of an ancient wisdom tradition originally presented in a text called the Book of Dzyan, which she described as "[a]n Archaic Manuscript – a collection of palm leaves made impermeable to water, fire, and air, by some specific unknown process" (Blavatsky 1888: vol. I: 1). The contents of this work, which nobody else has ever seen, written in a language – Senzar, whose existence is not documented in any other source – are a number of obscure stanzas which appear rendered into English in *The Secret Doctrine*.

Another imaginal or virtual foundational text referred to by a number of religious organizations is a purportedly ancient account of the life of Jesus that the Russian adventurer Nicolas Notovich (1858–1916) claimed to have come across in Ladakh in northernmost India. What readers of his *La vie inconnue de Jésus-Christ* (1894), in which its contents are summarized, are told is that Jesus, at the age of 13, left Palestine and traveled to India where he encountered representatives of all major Indian religions before returning to his homeland. This particular period in his life is not documented in any biblical text, and no evidence suggesting that the manuscript to which Notovich referred ever existed has surfaced. Skeptical voices sounded soon after the book was published, but the idea of Jesus having visited India proved to be attractive and has since the story's first appearance lived its own life.

In his summary of these lost years, Notovitch tells of how Jesus preached against both the caste system and polytheism, a message that did not endear him to his hosts. Some writers who have used the motif of Jesus' travels to India in their own works, however, have employed it to suggest that his true teachings were inspired by Asian religions. One notable example of this kind of shift is *The Aquarian Gospel of Jesus the Christ*, written by Levi Dowling (1844–1911) and published in 1908. Instead of crediting Notovitch as the originator of the claim, the contents of this particular volume are presented as a transcription from the Akashic records, a Theosophical concept denoting a source of revelatory knowledge.

After having received Dowling's Theosophically-tinged treatment, the legend was transposed to a new religion of a very different kind. It was integrated into the canonical text of the Moorish Science Temple of America, an influential African American religious movement. Large parts of *The Holy Koran of the Moorish Science Temple of America*, published in 1927, consist of what are lightly edited reproductions of sections of the *Aquarian Gospel*.[51] Significant points of divergence in this case include the omission of various sequences that appear in Dowling's book as well as referring to the deity as Allah rather than God. Versions of the same legend have been appropriated by other authors and movements, including Nicholas Roerich (1874–1947), co-founder of a member of the Theosophical family of religions called Agni Yoga, Swami Abhedananda (1866–1939) of the Ramakrishna movement, and Elizabeth Clare Prophet (1939–2009) of the Church Universal and Triumphant. Prophet writes at length on this topic in *The Lost Years of Jesus* (1984), a book that traces its claims back to Notovitch's account and argues that a manuscript indeed was discovered in Ladakh.

Texts as Material Objects

Texts primarily exist as material objects, that is, as handwritten scrolls or manuscripts, in printed form, as recordings, and depending upon how the term "material" is defined, as computer files. Religious texts, when in print, have all the physical characteristics of other similarly produced materials. Many are manufactured and distributed by companies that function just like any other market-oriented business does. They can be purchased from online retailers like Amazon that also sell other products. In the case of most books disseminated by NRMs or people within the looser cultic milieu, there are no generally shared sets of rules that govern how they are to be treated. They can be unceremoniously dumped in the trash if the owner wishes to do so, a fate that would be practically unthinkable for books central to many of the historically more established religions. Compared to the highly regulated and ritualized set of behaviors that develop around some of the more traditional sacred texts, Torah

---

[51] The text of *The Holy Koran of the Moorish Science Temple* is reproduced at https://hermetic .com/moorish/7koran.

scrolls, and copies of the Qur'an being particularly striking examples, most modern religious texts are thus allotted a rather modest degree of special treatment. There are, nonetheless, examples of such texts that are surrounded with an air of being in some respect qualitatively distinct from secular works.

One way of setting a text apart from other books is to make it visually similar to widely known sacred texts. Volumes like the Book of Mormon and Dowling's *Aquarian Gospel*, for instance, are produced in such a way so as to resemble Bible translations and thus project a sacred ethos different from that of works whose pages look like those of any other book. Widely available editions are printed with two columns per page, and brief summaries in italic font introduce numbered chapters. The style and structure of both books, and especially of the Book of Mormon, match the standard biblical format. Both are written in archaizing styles that depart significantly from contemporary forms of English. The Book of Mormon, in particular, is characterized by its unusual use of language, an impression resulting from its linguistic similarity to the King James Bible and the frequent appearance of formulaic expressions such as "And it came to pass." Whereas the *Aquarian Gospel* consists of twenty-two parts with the secular-sounding headings Section I to Section XXII, the division of the Book of Mormon into units given names like First Book of Nephi, Book of Helaman, and Book of Ether adds a further hint of it being scriptural.

Another way of setting a text deemed sacred apart from secular literature is to treat it in a reverential and ritualized fashion, for instance by reciting passages in a language attributed a sacred status within a religious community and in a particular manner that differs significantly from normal speech. Taylor (2015) discusses the way in which the Sanskrit text of the Bhagavata Purana is read aloud within the ISKCON movement (a milieu where it has canonical status as the most accurate account of the life of Krishna), despite the fact that few of its members have the knowledge necessary for actually understanding what is being said. That there is an ambition to allow those who are listening to understand the meaning of the recitation is apparent from the fact that recitations are often accompanied by interpretations provided in a vernacular language. Ritual efficacy, however, depends on having passages from the work recited by a person in authority, in a setting that is specially designated for the occasion, in the presence of an appropriate audience, and not least in Sanskrit, which here functions as a sacred language. Thus, the readings of the Bhagavata Purana function in a way similar to the pre–Vatican II Latin Mass in the Roman Catholic Church, along with the recitation of the Holy Qur'an in Arabic to non-Arabic-speaking congregations.

Analogous to the way in which Muslims treat the Qur'an in Arabic as the authentic text that no translation can really render, some NRMs treat the original version in which their central texts were composed or revealed as imbued with a sacrosanct quality that other renditions do not have. The original version can be understood as an exact reproduction of the language of the original text without any editorial changes whatsoever. The Danish prophet Martinus that we introduced earlier (see Section 3) wrote a sizeable corpus of texts over the course of many years, in which he presented a complex set of doctrines that, according to people sympathetic to his message, derive from his having achieved a permanent state of cosmic consciousness. During the long period of time within which these texts were written, a spelling reform was introduced in Denmark, which gives older works a certain aura of venerable age. Since 2005, a debate has raged within the Martinus milieu regarding whether new editions of older works can be published using modern spelling, and some opponents of the idea have referred to the unrevised texts as "the only real thing" and "sacred."[52] The concept of an unchanged text can refer not only to the language but even to the shape of the handwriting in the original manuscript. The occultist and founder of the religion of Thelema Aleister Crowley (1875–1947) claimed to have received the first, foundational text of the new religion in 1904, when a voice belonging to Aiwass, a messenger of the Egyptian god Horus, dictated a message that came to be known as *Liber AL vel Legis* or *Book of the Law*. A self-referential passage in the text (III:47) explains that "This book shall be translated into all tongues: but always with the original in the writing of the Beast [i.e., Crowley]; for in the chance shape of the letters and their position to one another: in these are mysteries that no Beast shall divine." The Ordo Templi Orientis (OTO), of which Crowley was leader from 1925 until his death, regards the *Book of the Law* as a central religious text that needs to be treated in accordance with these instructions. A passage printed on the dust jacket of the Swedish translation published by that organization (Anon 2014) exhorts the reader to consult the English text since any translation is an interpretation. Furthermore, roughly half of the book's pages consist of photographic reproductions of every page of the original manuscript in Crowley's handwriting.

At the most extreme point on a spectrum of distinctiveness, so to speak, we find texts revered by religious movements perceived as being utterly different from everything that we might call ordinary literature. Scientology, for instance, regards its founder, L. Ron Hubbard, as an unparalleled genius and has gone to extraordinary lengths to preserve his words for posterity. Newspaper reports have disclosed the existence of an underground vault at a remote location outside the small community of Trementina, New Mexico.[53] Here, copies of Hubbard's texts have been engraved on stainless steel tablets and encased in titanium capsules so that they will be preserved for all time. A gigantic version

---

[52] The debate is summarized in Christensen (2018).
[53] www.washingtonpost.com/wp-dyn/content/article/2005/11/26/AR2005112601065.html.

of a Scientology symbol has been bulldozed into the ground and is clearly visible on Google Maps. Hubbard's greatness and that of his texts are thus made manifest on the grandest of scales.

A new religious movement in the Buddhist family of traditions, Soka Gakkai, is known for a practice that highlights the sacrality of its most revered scripture in a unique way. Soka Gakkai was officially founded in Japan in 1930 and builds on a much earlier tradition, Nichiren Buddhism, one of several coexisting strands of Buddhism in Japan.[54] It shares with its mother tradition the reverence it holds for the Lotus Sutra, a Mahayana Buddhist text that is presented as a set of teachings going back to the historical Buddha but which was probably compiled in several stages, being given its final form at some unknown point in time in the first centuries of the Common Era. A characteristic teaching of Nichiren Buddhism and hence also of its modern successor Soka Gakkai is the conviction that the Lotus Sutra presents the final and most advanced version of the Buddha's teaching and that the title of the work contains the essence of the work itself. This core doctrine lies behind the practice of chanting a mantra that contains the name of the scripture, namely *namu myoho renge kyo*, "glory to the dharma of the Lotus Sutra," while seated in front of a *gohonzon*, a paper scroll decorated with a centrally placed calligraphic rendition of the mantra sur- rounded by the names of various Buddhas and bodhisattvas. The particular importance of the scroll does not lie in the meaning of the text reproduced on it but rather in its status as a religious object that, as one Soka Gakkai website puts it, "embodies the life of the original Buddha."[55] The soteriological significance of what the Lotus Sutra has to say is effectively transferred from the message communicated in the text via the text itself as an object of ritual devotion to a depiction of the title of the text rendered in a script that is unreadable for many members.

To summarize, the canonical texts of various new religions resemble those of more traditional religions in many ways. They present the teachings of these movements in an authoritative manner and are often legitimized in a secondary textual layer that explains why the canonical text is so extraordinary. Some movements go to great lengths to demonstrate how their sacred writings truly differ from other books, but, in general, it is hardly surprising that these volumes are sometimes treated in unceremonious ways since we are living in an era characterized by both a proliferation of texts and the mass distribution of printed matter.

---

[54] The history of the movement is rather more complicated than this statement would indicate (see Kisala 2004 for a history of Soka Gakkai), but these details are not relevant for the present purposes.

[55] https://sgi-vegas.org/intro-to-buddhism/gohonzon.

5 NRMs in Comparative Perspective

As we noted in the introduction, much of the early literature on NRMs saw the organizations that it studied in terms of the tension that characterized the relationships many groups had with their host societies. Most outsiders felt that these emergent movements were very different from what we might call more traditional religions, and therefore the nature and extent of these differences were central areas of research for NRM scholars. One of the main ideas informing this Element has been that people involved in newer and older religions alike create and disseminate myths, perform rituals, surround themselves with material objects, and relate to texts. Hence we have focused on areas where NRMs are quite similar to the more established religions of the host societies. This final section will largely be devoted to exploring some of the reasons for the existence of such similarities.

Our reasoning regarding why there are fundamental similarities between NRMs and more traditional religions has its basis in a cognitive approach to religion, which is built upon the idea that human brains and minds are the result of an evolutionary process and that various elements of what we call religion are products of that process. Since we all share the same evolutionary history, the religions that we produce will, of course, share the same basic traits. The cognitive science of religion is a vast and rapidly expanding field, and our ambition here is merely to give four basic examples of its explanatory power.[56] Briefly, we will look at how new as well as old religions provide ways of categorizing the impressions we receive, how we attribute human characteristics to the postulated denizens of suprahuman realms, how the fear of contagion influences religious concepts and behaviors, and how the limitations of our memories influence the shapes that religion can take.

The universal becomes specific and local when it is expressed in a particular social and historical context by people living in a particular kind of ecological niche with a particular economic system. Both hunter-gatherers and modern Americans and Europeans may craft and disseminate myths, but the hunter dwelling in the Kalahari Desert is rooted in an environment with conditions that differ greatly from those shaping the life of a twenty-first-century evangelical American or Scientologist, so the contents of the stories they tell will obviously be very different. Although the purpose of this Element is to explore questions other than those that have occupied most sociologically oriented studies of NRMs, approaches stemming from the comparative study of religions should not be seen as being divorced from social science-based perspectives. In the last

---

[56] Surveys of the cognitive science of religion (CSR) that cover a far vaster range of topics than we do here include Newen, De Bruin & Gallagher (2018), White (2021), and Barrett (2022).

part of this section, we will briefly return to the issue of context-bound differences between NRMs and older religions.

Classifying Impressions into Categories

We constantly receive and interpret a vast number of sensory impressions. The sights, sounds, and other stimuli that reach us would overwhelm us if we did not have cognitive shortcuts that allow us to understand our surroundings almost instantly and with no apparent intellectual effort. We sort impressions into mental categories without usually even being aware of doing so, and we base much of our day-to-day existence on such categories. Our representation of the category "dog," for instance, enables us to infer that a particular animal that we have never encountered before will probably be friendly toward us, but that one should perhaps keep a cautious distance because some dogs can be aggressive. The "dog" category contrasts with others, such as the category "cat," whose members we will, without much reflection, treat differently. Religions can play an important role in providing us with culturally produced categories, some of which are rather more problematic than the examples of familiar pets that we just gave. If we live in a cultural environment where a basic distinction is made between true believers and everybody else, such a categorization will have significant effects on one's behavior in everyday life. NRMs that postulate that this divide is fundamental and absolute can provide members with just such a cognitive shortcut that primes them to associate with one category and shun the other.

A very basic, and for religions presumably universal, way of dividing up the impressions that we form of our surroundings is one that we have alluded to before: the distinction between a category of what, in the terminology of Ann Taves (2009), is special from what is ordinary. As we have noted in the preceding section, the sacred texts of a religion are, in terms of their material shape, often to be found in the shape of books. A Bible and a copy of *Moby Dick* are essentially two towering stacks of printed pages sandwiched between a front and back cover. What distinguishes these volumes from each other is not so much the physical properties of the two material objects but rather the differential treatment given to them by people who attribute a specialness to the Bible that they do not feel the copy of *Moby Dick* possesses. Under particular circumstances – for instance, ritualized study sessions, or when experiencing a need for consolation or guidance – people who feel a connection with Christianity may consult the former but almost certainly not the latter. They might view the former as being divinely inspired or even inerrant, while the latter will be seen, at best, as a great work of fiction.

We remarked in the section on material objects that anything can potentially be given religious significance, and examples of seemingly quite everyday objects imbued with specialness indeed abound. What an outside observer with no cultural insight whatsoever into Christianity might see as just two pieces of wood fastened together at right angles is from an insider's perspective a cross, one of the most iconic and special symbols of the various Christian traditions. Very commonly, however, it is the visually striking that is set apart. We also observed in that section that various stones are treated as special by being attributed spiritual properties. What these stones have in common is that they have what cognitive anthropologist Pascal Boyer has characterized as a minimally counterintuitive property (Boyer 1994). Most, or at least a great many, stones are rather drab and unremarkable. The countless tiny pebbles and large hunks of grey rock many of us encounter on a daily basis generally do not attract our attention in any significant way, and our experience of stones as stones provides us with some kind of stock idea of what these objects are like in general. Amethysts, rose quartz, and snowflake obsidian, to mention just three of the many varieties commonly sold in New Age bookshops, are, we might say, just like ordinary pebbles in the sense that they are hard, inert objects found in nature. What sets them apart from more humdrum specimens is that they possess a striking, counterintuitive feature: their glossy and colored surfaces. The hypothesis that it is precisely this quality that makes them the focus of religious speculation is strengthened by the fact that, in addition to the beliefs about stones that abound in the contemporary West, we also find older, historically seemingly unrelated, traditions about the magical and healing properties of stones, and that these, too, are characterized by their focus on stones with extraordinary properties. Besides strikingly colored minerals, such traditions from antiquity focus on the seemingly mysterious properties of magnetic iron, for instance. While magnets are everyday objects for most of us, for the ancient Greeks, stones that had the inexplicable ability to draw other pieces of iron ore to them were singled out as special.

Anthropomorphism

It seems that people have a natural tendency to assume that there are human-like entities, such as spirits and gods, that interact with us and whose actions help explain what happens in our world.[57] Some versions of major religious traditions insist upon the utter transcendence of the deity and the sheer impossibility of describing its nature in human terms. These, however, are

---

[57] For a discussion based on cognitive psychology of this tendency to see suprahuman beings in anthropomorphic terms, see Shaman, Saide, & Richert (2019).

typically theologically elite understandings. The vast majority of members of any religious community either perceive of gods, spirits, and other suprahuman beings as having minds that largely function like our own human minds, as resembling us physically, or as having both of these qualities. We see this, for instance, in notions of gods having a range of emotions similar to ours. They may become angry or jealous when other gods are worshipped, and they are happy and content when sacrifices are offered to them. Descriptions of the denizens of the suprahuman realm also commonly focus on their corporeality which is often much like our own. In Christian traditions, iconographic representations and verbal descriptions of God are, despite the theological insistence on their inadequacy, often human, angels are like people with wings, and the devil is like a human with horns and hoofs. NRMs that expand upon the range of suprahuman beings encountered in mainstream Christianity continue to endow these entities with humanlike characteristics. UFO-based religions can serve as a case in point. Although actual beings from outer space, we may assume, would likely come in shapes completely unfamiliar to us, the imagined versions of inhabitants of distant planets we find in books, films, and other forms of media are typically humanoid. The suprahuman beings postulated by the Raëlian movement, the Elohim, are even described as "human scientists from another planet."[58] Within Raëlianism the similarity between the Elohim and ourselves is explained by referring to the statement in Genesis (1:26) that humans were created "in our likeness." What in many Jewish and Christian interpretations is treated as a statement made by the deity using a grammatical plural is here read as an allusion to a process of cloning carried out by extraterrestrial scientists who create the first humans to resemble them. As we saw in the earlier section on iconography, the culturally most widespread representation of what beings from outer space may look like depicts them as smallish, grey humanoid creatures with dark, slanted eyes. Books such as Whitley Strieber's bestselling *Communion*, modern folklore that promotes the idea that beings matching this description crashed a spaceship near Roswell, New Mexico, and movies like *Close Encounters of the Third Kind* have cemented the image of this particular figure in the popular imagination.

Contamination, Purity, and Food Taboos

Since it is biologically adaptive for humans to avoid contamination, evolution has hardwired a drive in us to avoid sources of potential pollution (Feder 2016). Pollution can mean dirt and germs in the most literal sense:

---

[58] https://raelusa.org/raelian-movement/.

there is a reason why we have developed a keen sense of smell for detecting illness-inducing items such as rotting food. More relevant for the study of religion, many religions have rules, some more elaborate than others, restricting contact with certain categories of people or animals and prohibiting the consumption of certain foods. Indian caste purity rules are examples of this, as are the numerous purity regulations and food taboos listed in the Hebrew Bible. In NRMs, the phenomenon is most prominent in movements having historical origins in traditions where such strictures against impurity occupy a central position. A so-called sattvic diet plays an important role in ISKCON, and food prepared according to the restrictions prescribed must not contain, among other ingredients, such items as meat, fish, eggs, onions, and mushrooms. The term "sattvic" refers to a way of classifying foodstuffs that is linked to the Indian tradition of Ayurveda and according to which three different "qualities" or *doshas* are present in a particular proportion in the body. What a person ought to drink and eat is here determined by the balance, or lack thereof, of these qualities. The body, in this view, is in an optimal state when a finely tuned equilibrium is maintained, and various kinds of food can in some movements that ultimately have historical roots in an Indian cultural context be seen as a potential cause of illness (Transcendental Meditation) or considered so polluting they need to be avoided entirely (ISKCON).

Diets of other types abound in the modern West and can hover in a grey area where religious conceptions of how the body functions and how different diets influence health coexist with ideas that have no obvious religious or spiritual point of reference. One fad diet among what would be many potential examples of this phenomenon is based on a modern classificatory system that has some structural similarities with the *dosha* concept of Ayurvedic medicine, namely, the blood type diet. According to its proponents, people can be classified into distinct categories measurable in terms of whether they have blood type A, B, AB, or O, and that what they eat ought to be determined by this placement. The blood type diet, contrary to Ayurvedic conceptions, is not framed in terms that are in any way spiritual. Cognitively universal themes like the avoidance of pollution and the desire to classify the world around us are, of course, expressed in specific ways depending on the cultural context. Due to the enormous rhetorical force that the sciences have accrued in the modern world, there is a widespread tendency to legitimize one's ideas by referring to their purported scientific validity. The underlying rationale of the blood type diet – one that is rejected as pseudoscientific by the scientific mainstream – is that a particular class of proteins gets digested differently by individuals with different blood types.

The Role of Memory

Memory is crucial for the existence of religion. Members of a given tradition can only distinguish between the ordinary and the sacred if they are able to remember which is which, can only speculate on the characteristics of the postulated suprahuman entities if they can remember who these entities are, and can only follow rules of ritual purity if they can recall what the rules require. In modern societies, written accounts can, of course, supplement memory, but the importance of human memory becomes especially clear when one considers the challenge of transmitting religious knowledge to the next generation. Children need to commit at least basic religious information to memory in order for the religion to be passed on to the next generation. A theory of religion formulated by Harvey Whitehouse, distinguishes two types of religion that depend on distinct forms of memory (Whitehouse 2000, 2004).

Episodic memory stores single, salient events. We remember specific details from our last birthday or what we were doing when we first heard about the attacks on 9/11. Semantic memory allows us to recall general knowledge, procedures, and routines. This is what allows us to remember as a general fact that Moscow is the capital of Russia and makes us able to easily recall what we usually eat for breakfast. The two forms of memory we have briefly described here correspond to what Whitehouse calls imagistic religiosity, which depends on salient events, and doctrinal religiosity, which relies on the ability to memorize general knowledge about one's religious tradition.

Imagistic religion is intensely emotional, rituals of initiation being prototypical examples. In order to succeed in creating this emotional atmosphere, the groups that participate cannot be too large, and, for the emotion to be sufficiently intense, the experience must not be repeated too often. Rituals that mark the passage from one grade to the next in multi-tier initiatory organizations are examples of the imagistic mode. The newcomer to the Ordo Templi Orientis can be given the opportunity to pass a first threshold by participating as a character in an elaborate, symbolic drama, the details of which are kept secret from outsiders. Doctrinal religiosity is the converse of the imagistic kind. The details of doctrines and rituals are deemed to be very important and require considerable work to commit to memory. Rote learning or frequent participation in communal rituals is typical of such religions. Examples of NRMs with doctrinal characteristics are ubiquitous: religions as diverse as Scientology and ISKCON can be seen as never-ending explorations of vast corpora of knowledge.

What imagistic and doctrinal modes of religion share is the need for a leadership to stage the intense rituals or provide the occasions for learning the detailed doctrines and rituals. Religious milieus of a more unstructured type rely on a baseline of what is cognitively optimal.[59] By corresponding to ways of thinking and acting that in some sense feel "natural" to people, such forms of religion get passed on and committed to memory without the need for a hierarchy of religious leaders. One such natural tendency is to see patterns in events. Our ability to see patterns and draw causal conclusions is crucial: without it, we would not be able to understand our environment and make rational decisions. If we see dark clouds, we may draw the conclusion that it will soon rain, and a suitable response might be to carry an umbrella or even to stay indoors. A sizeable body of research, however, indicates that we tend to see causal connections whether or not there are any. Many New Age practices hinge on perceiving such patterns and connections. Divinatory systems such as astrology and the tarot are constructed around the propensity to see a link between a set of symbols – the various planets, signs, and angles of a chart, or cards picked at random from a deck – and the narrative that in the divinatory situation is being constructed about the life of the person for whom the reading is done. If the narrative feels like a good fit, this will convince the diviner's clients that the ritual itself works: the astrological interpretation feels right, not because the astrologer is good at reading people or because the client has revealed a lot about themselves, but because the symbols on the chart actually do reflect a correspondence between celestial and terrestrial events.

Expressing the Universal in a Modern Context

Although a cognitive approach to religion can go a long way toward explaining why religions resemble each other in fundamental ways, it is equally true that specific religions are produced within specific historical and cultural contexts and will only seem meaningful and relevant to their adherents if they reflect those contexts. We end this section by sketching four of the many ways in which new religions that have arisen in the West have found ways to adapt to such fundamental traits of their host societies as the dominant position of the sciences, the coexistence of many religious and secular options, an increasingly individualistic ethos, and the demands inherent in a capitalist economy.

Centuries ago, scientific advances in understanding the natural world could be rendered legitimate by claiming that God had authored two "books," namely the Bible and nature, and that exploring the latter was a way of understanding the divine order. The tables have since turned and as several of our examples in this Element illustrate, references to science are very common in the myths of new religions (see, e.g., Bigliardi 2023). The creation myths of the Nation of

---

[59] The concept of cognitive optimality in religion is discussed in Boyer (1994) and has been a point of departure of much research in the cognitive science of religion.

Islam and of Raëlianism differ fundamentally from each other, but both are predicated on being scientifically valid. The invocation of science has been a mainstay of religious innovation since the nineteenth century, and over time, widely accepted scientific views have, of course, changed dramatically. Helena Blavatsky argued in *The Secret Doctrine* (cf. Blavatsky 1888: vol I, 549) that the cosmology expounded in her book was compatible with modern science, and Fritjof Capra (b. 1939) made an analogous claim nearly a century later in *The Tao of Physics* (1975). For Blavatsky, modern science comprised a view of the world where atoms are the smallest, indivisible particles of matter and where the void is filled with a subtle ether, whereas Capra's science dispenses with the concept of ether and presupposes that atoms are divisible and that there is a significant array of different subatomic particles.

Being scientific is so important in the eyes of the adherents of some NRMs they vehemently reject the label religion. Anthroposophy, for instance, was founded by a charismatic leader whose status is based on claims of having direct insight into a normally invisible, spiritual dimension of existence, a plethora of culturally postulated suprahuman beings that are said to influence our lives, concepts of an afterlife, canonical texts, and a gamut of rituals. Many Anthroposophists nevertheless describe their movement as a science or a path toward knowledge and, when asked, deny that Anthroposophy is a religious movement.

Although the sciences have an unparalleled rhetorical power and thus argu-ably represent the most important competitor to any new religion, the modern world is characterized by a fragmented religious landscape and a multitude of competing worldviews, a fact that spokespersons for new religions are aware of and attempt to deal with in various ways. Novel religions have two basic choices when faced with the mosaic of coexisting and competing possibilities: they can declare themselves to be the only set of teachings that represents the truth, or they can argue that other religions have some valid elements.

Both choices come in many varieties. It is perfectly possible for members of religions that claim to hold the exclusive keys to salvation to express this conviction in muted terms: both authors of the present Element have for instance had numerous exchanges with the Jehovah's Witnesses, whose persua-sion that they alone will be saved has certainly not prevented them from being truly pleasant conversation partners. Other groups, such as the Westboro Baptist Church, mentioned earlier (see Section 2), have become notorious for their vocal condemnation of all outsiders.

Religions that argue that many, perhaps even all, religious traditions contain an element of truth are faced with the fact that religions differ immensely on any number of points. One way to meet this challenge is via the perennialist trope that although truth is found everywhere, their own version of it is superior. Theosophy, as well as various religions that have their historical roots in the Theosophical current, argue that religions present two aspects. There is an exoteric aspect that is the form of religion that most people are aware of and follow, and there is an esoteric aspect known only to individuals who have reached a higher spiritual state. Exoteric forms of the major religions of the world differ in numerous ways, but the esoteric core is said to be identical to them all.

The fragmentation of the religious landscape is exacerbated by the individualistic ethos of modern, Western societies. Just as most people in the modern West agree that we should be allowed to have a decisive voice in deciding what career we wish to pursue, where we decide to live, and with whom, religious interest and affiliation also tend to be presented as matters of individual choice. In this perspective, even the very term religion can be associated with blind faith in dogmas or allegiance to a hierarchically organized movement, whereas a term such as spirituality has more positive connotations. Individualism is particularly cultivated in New Age milieus. According to this individualistic norm, we are supposed to choose what rings true to our hearts. Subjectivity, intuition, and feeling are presented as the best ways to gain spiritual insight.

Individualism should, however, be understood as a norm rather than as an unproblematic fact (cf. Hammer 2010). After even a brief acquaintance with the New Age milieu, one will recognize a certain type of aesthetics, a particular way of expressing oneself. New Age bookshops all over the world are strikingly similar: the same muted music is played in the background as customers navigate between shelves carrying the same range of books and displays presenting the same crystals, essential oils, posters, packs of incense, and figurines. The rituals and doctrinal elements that are presented in most of the New Age literature are also quite homogeneous. Whereas the historical and anthropological literature documents a dazzling range of methods of divination, only half a dozen or so have any substantial following in the New Age milieu. Of all the potential answers to the question of life after death, only one has attracted any sustained interest: reincarnation, in an optimistic model that presupposes that we learn and grow from one incarnation to the next. Despite the insistence on individual choice, the fundamental psychological urge to belong to a group and adapt to its norms characterizes much of what is on offer.

The other side of the same coin is that religious movements are subjected to the same financial constraints that all organizations face in the modern world. To put it in stark terms: if they cannot generate enough income, the bills will not get paid. If they wish to survive, they need to adapt to the market and provide a product that can attract customers. If what they offer is perceived as radically unfamiliar and appeals to too few people to ensure funding for their day-to-day operations, they will ultimately, and unsurprisingly, cease to exist.

The need, or desire, to accumulate revenue is, of course, nothing new. Any religion that has fulltime specialists, whether Buddhist monks or Christian clergy, requires resources to be set apart so that some people can devote themselves to serving the organization. Depending on the economic system within which a religious community operates, the necessary funds can be generated through a variety of ways: donations, taxes, the sale of products, volunteer commitment, or, in older times, slave labor and looting the property of nonmembers. Quite a few new religions have adapted to the global capitalist economy and have become commercialized in the sense that what they offer is treated as saleable commodities. In some cases, the movement's teachings and rituals are the main commodity: Scientology is known for the price tags attached to most of its courses. In others, the material products of the religion are its main merchandise. Anthroposophy is an example of a religious movement that has developed a particularly broad product range. There are Anthroposophically produced foodstuffs (biodynamic products) and Anthroposophical cosmetics (marketed under such brand names as Weleda), whose customer base reaches well beyond the confines of those who would identify as Anthroposophists. Biodynamic wines, for instance, are trendy among consumers who may be completely unaware of the ritualized form of farming that has gone into producing the product and who may believe that these are basically identical to organic wines.

New religions arise within a particular social context and although they are typically presented as alternatives to the dominant social order, their otherness will be shaped by the norms of the host society: a religion that departed too radically from these norms would no doubt find it very difficult to gain adherents. The movements described in this Element overwhelmingly come from Western Europe and North America, where the factors we have described – the rhetorical force of science, a fragmented religious landscape, individualism, and the pervasive influence of the market economy – exert a powerful influence on emergent religions. A few and admittedly anecdotal examples from other parts of the globe confirm the basic tenet that religions, although they resemble each other in fundamental ways, reflect their own cultural settings. Homegrown Russian religions that emerged in the chaos following the dissolution of the Soviet Union were characterized by their apocalypticism (Shterin 2012); NRMs in Africa tend to deal with themes such as colonialism and the legacy of precolonial African traditions (Clarke 2012); and some movements that have been transplanted to Israel have adapted to the militarized social order there (Ben-Porat & Huss 2023). Since the turn of the twenty-first century, and in particular after the publication of two seminal texts by sociologist Shmuel Eisenstadt (2000a, 2000b), the social scientific exploration of modernity has been profoundly influenced by the insight that the processes of modernization take distinct shapes in various parts of the world. Scholarship on a truly global range of NRMs that combines approaches from the comparative study of religion with those of the social sciences will be crucial in shedding light on the ways in which emergent religions on the one hand display shared traits grounded in the evolutionary history of our species and on the other reflect the specific characteristics of multiple modernities.

References

Anon. 2014. *Lagens Bok. Liber AL vel Legis*. Stockholm: Ordo Templi Orientis Sverige.

Ansari, Z. I. 1981. Aspects of Black Muslim Theology. *Studia Islamica* 53: 137–76.

Ashcraft, W. M. 2018. *A Historical Introduction to the Study of New Religious Movements*. London: Routledge.

Athay, R. G. 1968. Worlds Without Number: The Astronomy of Enoch, Abraham, and Moses. *BYU Studies Quarterly* 8: 255–69.

Bailey, A. 1949. *The Destiny of the Nations*. New York: Lucis Trust.

Barrett, J. L. 2022. *Oxford Handbook of the Cognitive Science of Religion*. New York: Oxford University Press.

Barret-Fox, R. 2016. *God Hates: Westboro Baptist Church, American Nationalism, and the Religious Right*. Lawrence, KS: University Press of Kansas.

Bascom, W. A. 1965. The Forms of Folklore: Prose Narratives. *Journal of American Folklore* 78: 3–20.

Bell, C. 2009a. *Ritual: Perspectives and Dimensions*. 2nd ed. New York: Oxford University Press.

Bell, C. 2009b. *Ritual Theory. Ritual Practice*. 2nd ed. New York: Oxford University Press.

Ben-Porat, G. & B. Huss. 2023. Fighting for Legitimacy: New Religious Movements and Militarism in Israel. *Nova Religio* 26(3): 80–100.

Besant, A. 1905. *Esoteric Christianity: The Lesser Mysteries*. 2nd ed. London: J. Lane (with numerous reprints).

Bigliardi, S. 2023. *New Religious Movements and Science*. Cambridge: Cambridge University Press.

Blavatsky, H. 1888. *The Secret Doctrine*. New York: Theosophical University Press (with numerous reprints).

Boyer, P. 1994. *The Naturalness of Religious Ideas*. Berkeley: University of California Press.

Bromley, D. G. 2009. Making Sense of Scientology: Prophetic, Contractual Religion. In J. R. Lewis, ed. *Scientology*. Oxford: Oxford University Press, pp. 83–101.

Brown, F. 1997. *The Channeling Zone: American Spirituality in an Anxious Age*. Cambridge, MA: Harvard University Press.

Burt, A. R. 2023. *Hare Krishna in the Twenty-First Century*. Cambridge: Cambridge University Press.

Campbell, C. 1972. The Cult, the Cultic Milieu and Secularization. In M. Hill, ed. *A Sociological Yearbook of Religion in Britain*. London: SCM Press, pp. 119–36.

Capra, F. 1975. *The Tao of Physics: An Exploration of the Parallels Between Modern Physics and Eastern Mysticism*. Boulder, CO: Shambhala Publications.

Christensen, J. K. 2014. Sprogbersærkernes retskrivningsstrid. *Kosmos* 3: 77–80.

Chryssides, G. 1999. *Exploring New Religions*. London: Continuum.

Clarke, P. 2012. New Religious Movements in Sub-Saharan Africa. In O. Hammer & M. Rothstein, eds. *The Cambridge Companion to New Religious Movements*. Cambridge: Cambridge University Press, pp. 303–20.

Davis, R. H. 2015. *The Bhagavad Gita: A Biography*. Princeton: Princeton University Press.

Denzler, B. 2003. *The Lure of the Edge: Scientific Passions, Religious Beliefs, and the Pursuit of UFOs*. Berkeley, CA: University of California Press.

Dowling, L. 1908. *The Aquarian Gospel of Jesus the Christ*. Los Angeles: Leo W. Dowling (with numerous reprints).

Dubuisson, D. 2014. *Twentieth-Century Mythologies: Dumézil, Lévi-Strauss, Eliade*. Revised ed. Abingdon: Routledge.

Eisenstadt, S. 2000a. Multiple Modernities. *Daedalus* 129(1): 1–29.

Eisenstadt, S. 2000b. The Reconstruction of Religious Arenas in the Framework of "Multiple Modernities." *Millennium: Journal of International Studies* 29(3): 591–611.

Fäth, R. J. & David V. (eds.). 2015. *ænigma: One Hundred Years of Anthroposophical Art*. Prague: Arbor Vitae.

Feder, Y. 2016. Contamination Appraisals, Pollution Beliefs, and the Role of Cultural Inheritance in Shaping Disease Avoidance Behavior. *Cognitive Science* 40(6): 1561–85.

Ferguson, M. 1980. *The Aquarian Conspiracy: Personal and Social Transformation in the 1980s*. New York: Tarcher.

Firestone, R. 2012. "Jihadism" as a New Religious Movement. In O. Hammer & M. Rothstein, eds. *The Cambridge Companion to New Religious Movements*. Cambridge: Cambridge University Press, pp. 261–85.

Fuller, J. G. 1966. *The Interrupted Journey: Two Lost Hours "Aboard a Flying Saucer."* New York: Dial Press (with numerous reprints).

Gallagher, E. 2014. *Reading and Writing Scripture in New Religious Movements: New Bibles and New Revelations*. New York: Palgrave/ Macmillan.

Gardell, M. 1996. *In the Name of Elijah Muhammad: Louis Farrakhan and the Nation of Islam*. Durham, NC: Duke University Press.

Garwood, C. 2007. *Flat Earth: The History of an Infamous Idea*. London: Macmillan.

Goswami, S. D. 1980. *Srila Prabhupada Lilamrta: A Biography of His Divine Grace A. C. Bhaktivedanta Swami Prabhupada*. 7 vols. Los Angeles: Bhaktivedanta Book Trust.

Green, M. 1990. Mau Mau Oathing Rituals and Political Ideology in Kenya: A Re-Analysis. *Africa: Journal of the International African Institute* 60(1): 69–87.

Grimes, R. 2000. Ritual. In W. Braun & R. T. McCutcheon, eds. *Guide to the Study of Religion*. London: Cassell, pp. 259–70.

Hammer, O. 2010. I Did It My Way? Individual Choice and Social Conformity in New Age Religion. In S. Aupers & D. Houtman, eds. *Religions of Modernity: Relocating the Sacred to the Self and the Digital*. Leiden: Brill, pp. 49–68.

Hammer, O. 2019. Occult Scriptural Exegesis: Theosophical Readings of the Bible. In B. E. Elness-Hanson & J. Skarpeid, eds. *A Critical Study of Classical Religious Texts in Global Contexts: Challenges of a Changing World*. New York: Peter Lang, pp. 153–66.

Hammer, O. & M. Rothstein. 2012. Canonical and Extracanonical Texts in New Religions. In O. Hammer & M. Rothstein, eds. *The Cambridge Companion to New Religious Movements*. Cambridge: Cambridge University Press, pp. 113–22.

Hammer, O. & M. Rothstein. 2023. *Religious Innovation in the Hellenistic and Roman Periods*. Cambridge: Cambridge University Press.

Hammer, O. & K. Swartz. 2020. The Bosnian Pyramid Phenomenon. *Nova Religio* 23(4): 94–110.

Hammer, O. & K. Swartz. 2021. Ancient Aliens. In B. E. Zeller, ed. *Handbook of UFO Religions*. Leiden: Brill, pp. 151–77.

Hammer, O. & K. Swartz. 2024. Graham Hancock. Prometheus for a New Age: Alternative Archaeology as Modern Mythmaking. *Nova Religio* 27: forthcoming.

Harvey, S. & S. Newcombe (eds.). 2013. *Prophecy in the New Millennium: When Prophecy Persists*. London: Routledge.

Hoopes, J. W. 2011. A Critical History of 2012 Mythology. In C. L. N. Ruggles, ed. *"Oxford IX" International Symposium on Archaeoastronomy Proceedings IAU Symposium No. 278*. Cambridge: Cambridge University Press, pp. 240–48.

Hutton, R. 2008. Modern Pagan Festivals: A Study in the Nature of Tradition. *Folklore* 119(3): 251–73.

Hutton, R. 2009. *Blood and Mistletoe: The History of Druids in Britain*. New Haven, CT: Yale University Press.

Introvigne, M. 2016. New Religious Movements and the Visual Arts. *Nova Religio*, 19(4): 3–13.

Introvigne, M. 2022. *Brainwashing*. Cambridge: Cambridge University Press.

Kisala, R. 2004. Soka Gakkai: Searching for the Mainstream. In J. R. Lewis & J. Aa. Petersen, eds. *Controversial New Religions*. Oxford: Oxford University Press, pp. 139–52.

Lévi-Strauss. C. 1966. *The Savage Mind*. Chicago: University of Chicago Press.

Lewis, J. R. 2003. *Legitimating New Religions*. New Brunswick, NJ: Rutgers University Press.

Lewis, J. R. 2016. Technological Exorcism, Body Thetans, and Scientology's Secret Mythology. *Numen* 63(1): 33–53.

Lincoln, B. 1999. *Theorizing Myth: Narrative, Ideology, and Scholarship*. Chicago: University of Chicago Press.

Lucas, P. C. 2011. New Age Millennialism. In C. Wessinger, ed. *The Oxford Handbook of Millennialism*. Oxford: Oxford University Press, pp. 567–86.

Lund, G. N. 1992. Plan of Salvation, Plan of Redemption. In D. H. Ludlow, ed. *Encyclopedia of Mormonism*. New York: Macmillan, pp. 1088–91. https://eom.byu.edu/index.php/Plan_of_Salvation,_Plan_of_Redemption.

MacLaren Walsh, J. & B. Topping. 2018. *The Man who Invented Aztec Crystal Skulls: The Adventures of Eugène Boban*. New York: Berghahn Books.

Malinowski, B. 1948 [1926]. Myth in Primitive Psychology. In B. Malinowski, ed. *Magic, Science and Religion and Other Essays*. Boston, MA: Beacon Press, pp. 72–124.

McCutcheon, R. T. 2000. Myth. In W. Braun & R. T. McCutcheon, eds. *Guide to the Study of Religion*. London: Cassell, pp. 190–208.

McGuire, M. 1988. *Ritual Healing in Suburban America*. New Brunswick, NJ: Rutgers University Press.

Melton, J. G. 2016. *Encyclopedia of American Religions*. 9th ed. Farmington Hills, MI: Gale Research.

Moerman, D. E. 2002. *Medicine, Meaning, and the Placebo Effect*. Cambridge: Cambridge University Press.

Morgan, D. 2010. Introduction: The Matter of Belief. In D. Morgan, ed. *Religion and Material Culture: The Matter of Belief*. London: Routledge, pp. 1–17.

Newen, A., L. De Bruin & S. Gallagher (eds.). 2018. *The Oxford Handbook of 4E Cognition*. Oxford: Oxford University Press.

Nielsen, K. F. & S. D. Ricks. 1992. Creation, Creation Accounts. In D. H. Ludlow, ed. *Encyclopedia of Mormonism*. New York: Macmillan, pp. 340–43. https://eom.byu.edu/index.php/Creation,_Creation_Accounts

Notovitch, N. 1894. *La vie inconnue de Jésus-Christ*. Paris: Paul Ollendorff (with numerous reprints).

Ohlenschläger, S. 1999. *Rudolf Steiner (1861–1925): Das architektonische Werk*. Petersberg: Michael Imhof Verlag.

Pace, E. 2000. Damanhur, de la religion à la politique. *Ethnologie française*, nouvelle série, 30(4): 575–82.

Palmer, S. J. 2004. *Aliens Adored: Rael's UFO Religion*. New Brunswick, NJ: Rutgers University Press.

Palmer, S. J. 2005. The Raelian Movement: Concocting Controversy, Seeking Social Legitimacy, In J. R. Lewis & J. Aa. Petersen, eds. *Controversial New Religions*. 2nd ed. New York: Oxford University Press, pp. 371–85.

Palmer, S. J. 2010. *The Nuwaubian Nation: Black Spirituality and State Control*. London: Routledge.

Paul, E. R. 1992. Astronomy, Scriptural References to. In D. H. Ludlow, ed. *Encyclopedia of Mormonism*. New York: Macmillan, p. 82. https://eom.byu.edu/index.php/Astronomy,_Scriptural_References_to.

Penton, M. J. 2015. *Apocalypse Delayed: The Story of Jehovah's Witnesses*. 3rd ed. Toronto: University of Toronto Press.

Pinkney, A. M. 2018. Prasāda. In K. A. Jacobsen (editor in chief). *Brill Encyclopedia of Hinduism Online*. Leiden: Brill.

Prophet, E. C. 1984. *The Lost Years of Jesus: On the Discoveries of Notovitch, Abhedananda, Roerich, and Caspari*. Livingston, MT: Summit University Press.

Rappaport, R. 1999. *Ritual and Religion in the Making of Humanity*. Cambridge: Cambridge University Press.

Rothstein, M. 2009. "And his Name was Xenu, He Used Renegades … ": Aspects of Scientology's Founding Myth. In J. R. Lewis, ed. *Scientology*. New York: Oxford University Press, pp. 365–87.

Rowbotham, S. B. 1881. *Zetetic Astronomy: Earth not a Globe*. 3d ed. London: n.p.

Schjødt, U., H. Stødkilde-Jørgensen, A. W. Geertz & A. Roepstorff. 2009. Highly Religious Participants Recruit Areas of Social Cognition in Personal Prayer. *Social Cognitive and Affective Neuroscience* 4(2): 199–207.

Schmidt, R. 2010. Membership – Study – Contact. In J. Kühl, B. von Plato, & H. Zimmermann, eds. *The School of Spiritual Science: An Orientation and Introduction*. Forest Row: Temple Lodge, pp. 96–100.

Segal, R. A. 2021. *Myth Analyzed*. Abingdon: Routledge.

Shaman, N. J., A. R. Saide & R. A. Richert. 2019. Dimensional Structure of and Variation in Anthropomorphic Concepts of God. In G. Airenti, M. Cruciani & A. Plebe, eds. *The Cognitive Underpinnings of Anthropomorphism*. Frontiers in Psychology. Lausanne: Frontiers Media, pp. 46–61.

Shterin, M. 2012. New Religious Movements in Changing Russia. In O. Hammer & M. Rothstein, eds. *The Cambridge Companion to New Religious Movements*. Cambridge: Cambridge University Press, pp. 286–307.

Simmel, G. 1992. Das Geheimnis und die geheime Gesellschaft. In G. Simmel, ed. *Soziologie: Untersuchungen über die Formen der Vergesellschaftung*. Frankfurt am Main: Suhrkamp, pp. 383–55.

Smith, J. Z. 1982. Sacred Persistence: Towards a Redescription of Canon. In J. Z. Smith, ed. *Imagining Religion: From Babylon to Jonestown*. Chicago: University of Chicago Press, pp. 36–52.

Strenski, I. 1987. *Four Theories of Myth in Twentieth-Century History: Cassirer, Eliade, Lévi-Strauss, and Malinowski*. London: Macmillan.

Taves, A. 2009. *Religious Experience Reconsidered: A Building Block Approach to the Study of Religion and Other Special Things*. Princeton: Princeton University Press.

Taves, A. 2016. *Revelatory Events: Three Case Studies of the Emergence of New Spiritual Paths*. Princeton: Princeton University Press.

Taylor, M. 2015. How to Do Things with Sanskrit: Speech Act Theory and the Oral Performance of Sacred Text. *Numen* 62(5/6): 519–37.

Urban, H. B. 2011. *The Church of Scientology: A History of a New Religion*. Princeton: Princeton University Press.

Urban, H. B. 2021. *Secrecy: Silence, Power, and Religion*. Chicago: University of Chicago Press.

Van Gennep, A. 1960 [1909]. *The Rites of Passage*. London: Routledge.

Vogel, D. 2021. *Book of Abraham Apologetics: A Review and Critique*. Salt Lake City, UT: Signature Books.

Vorilhon, C. (a.k.a Raël). 1974. *Le livre qui dit la vérité: le message donné par les extra-terrestres*. Clermont-Ferrand: L'édition du message.

Walsh, J. M. 2008. Legend of the Crystal Skulls: The Truth Behind Indiana Jones's Latest Quest. *Archaeology* 61: 36–41.

White, C. 2021. *An Introduction to the Cognitive Science of Religion*. London: Routledge.

Whitehouse, H. 2000. *Arguments and Icons: Divergent Modes of Religiosity*. Oxford: Oxford University Press.

Whitehouse, H. 2004. *Modes of Religiosity: A Cognitive Theory of Religious Transmission*. Walnut Creek, CA: Alta Mira Press.

Zander, H. 2007. *Anthroposophie in Deutschland: Theosophische Weltanschauung und gesellschaftliche Praxis 1884–1945*. Göttingen: Vandenhock & Ruprecht.

Zander, H. 2019. *Die Anthroposophie: Rudolf Steiners Ideen zwischen Esoterik, Weleda, Demeter und Waldorfpädagogik.* Paderborn: Schöningh.

Zeller, B. E. 2014. *Heaven's Gate: America's UFO Religion.* New York: New York University Press.

Zoccatelli, P. 2016. All the Heavens in your Hands. *Nova Religio* 19(4): 145–62.

Cambridge Elements ≡

New Religious Movements

Founding Editor

†James R. Lewis

Wuhan University

The late James R. Lewis was Professor of Philosophy at Wuhan University, China. He served as the editor or co-editor for four book series, was the general editor for the *Alternative Spirituality and Religion Review*, and the associate editor for the *Journal of Religion and Violence*. His publications include *The Cambridge Companion to Religion and Terrorism* (Cambridge University Press 2017) and *Falun Gong: Spiritual Warfare and Martyrdom* (Cambridge University Press 2018).

Series Editor

Rebecca Moore

San Diego State University

Rebecca Moore is Emerita Professor of Religious Studies at San Diego State University. She has written and edited numerous books and articles on Peoples Temple and the Jonestown tragedy. She has served as co-general editor or reviews editor of *Nova Religio* since 2000. Publications include *Beyond Brainwashing: Perspectives on Cult Violence* (Cambridge University Press 2018) and *Peoples Temple and Jonestown in the Twenty-First Century* (Cambridge University Press 2022).

About the Series

Elements in New Religious Movements go beyond cult stereotypes and popular prejudices to present new religions and their adherents in a scholarly and engaging manner. Case studies of individual groups, such as Transcendental Meditation and Scientology, provide in-depth consideration of some of the most well known, and controversial, groups. Thematic examinations of women, children, science, technology, and other topics focus on specific issues unique to these groups. Historical analyses locate new religions in specific religious, social, political, and cultural contexts. These examinations demonstrate why some groups exist in tension with the wider society and why others live peacefully in the mainstream. The series highlights the differences, as well as the similarities, within this great variety of religious expressions. To discuss contributing to this series please contact Professor Moore, remoore@sdsu.edu.

Cambridge Elements ═

New Religious Movements